City Walks of London

Edited by Paul Begg

Robson Books

This book is for Siobán and Judy Begg
and Barbara Galea

First published in Great Britain in 1990 by Robson Books Ltd,
Bolsover House, 5–6 Clipstone Street, London W1P 7EB

British Library Cataloguing in Publication Data
  City walks of London.
  I. Begg, Paul
  914.2104858

  ISBN 0 86051 647 4

Typeset by Bookworm Typesetting, Manchester
Printed in Great Britain by
Biddles Ltd., Guildford & King's Lynn

CONTENTS

ACKNOWLEDGEMENTS

On behalf of the contributors I would like to thank the staff of the many libraries whose help has always been invaluable. Also, on behalf of City Walks, the great many people whose enthusiasm has helped to make the tours a success.

I would personally like to express my gratitude to the contributors who somehow managed to find the time in their very busy schedules to write such entertaining chapters. I am reluctant to single out any individual, for everyone deserves equal praise, but special thanks must go to Roger Tyrrell, who not only contributed three excellent chapters, but otherwise proved a dedicated and enthusiastic helpmate on this project. The book deservedly owes much to him.

Finally, thanks, too, to Robson Books and City Walks who made this book possible. Both have remained enthusiastic during some trying moments.

Paul Begg
Leeds, 1990

INTRODUCTION
Paul Begg

Called *Londinium* by the Romans, *Lundene* by the Saxons, London has a history which stretches over almost 2,000 years. It may be imagined that successive disasters – the Great Fire of 1666, the Blitz of World War Two, and the ravages of modern development – have left little of this history to be seen on the streets. This is not the case. As one of the contributors to this book says, the very layout of London's streets has its origins in the distant past, a past which can be summoned to the forefront of the mind's eye by no more than a street name.

The history of London is to be found up the side streets and down the alleys, passages and lanes, in places which the casual visitor may not penetrate. One way of visiting these places is on a walking tour. One of the most successful, and arguably the best walking tour company in London, is City Walks. This is in no small part due to the quality of City Walks guides. They have not learned their subject from a script. They do not respond to questions with incomprehension and ignorance. The guides, as this book demonstrates, have a deep knowledge and love of their subjects. They have not only read widely, gaining a fund of anecdotes in the process; most have conducted original research, unearthing new and little known information.

This book is based on six City Walks tours. It is not a guide book, although any visitor to London will certainly find that this book will guide them to some fascinating places, but a thematic history of a part or period of London history. It is varied in content and takes the reader from the foundation of London by the Romans to the terrible destruction caused by the Blitz.

Colin Oakes takes us into the streets off St Paul's Cathedral. He points out a small memorial set into the wall of Panyer Alley, near St Paul's Underground Station. The inscription on this memorial returns us to the foundation of London by the Romans, by either Emperor Claudius (AD 41−54) or Emperor Nero (AD 54−68). The Roman writer Tacitus wrote of the original Roman London that it 'did not rank as a Roman settlement, but was an important centre for businessmen and merchandise.' This original community was razed by two rebellious British tribes led by Queen Boudicca in AD 60. Dio Cassius described her thus: 'In stature she was very tall and grim in appearance, with a piercing gaze and a harsh voice. She had a mass of very fair hair which grew down to her hips.' Tacitus estimated that her rebellion cost the lives of 70,000 people.

Although she was defeated, Boudicca came within an ace of overturning the might of the Romans. Dio Cassius says that the Britons gave her a rich burial, a tantalizing piece of information for the archaeologist. A bronze statue of Boudicca and her daughters now stands on the Thames Embankment.

According to tradition Roman Britain came to an end in AD 410. Over the next 400 years or so various Germanic tribes, today collectively called Anglo-Saxons, began to settle and establish kingdoms in Britain. Traditionally the first such kingdom was Kent, its founders being called Hengest and Horsa. The *Anglo-Saxon Chronicle* records that in 457 Hengest defeated the Britons at *Crecganford* (Crayford, Kent) and that the Britons 'fled to London in Great Terror.' This is the last literary reference to London for 200 years. It is not known whether London continued to be occupied or not, but the Saxons appear to have avoided it and settled outside the walls.

London is next heard of in 601 with the consecration of the first bishop of London and the subsequent construction of St Paul's. This brings us back to Colin Oakes' 'Secret City', for St Paul's not only united the old Roman city of London with the Anglo-Saxon trading centre outside the walls, it influenced much of the activities in the streets surrounding the cathedral. Colin recites the history of those streets, the religious communities who lived in them and the changes which have taken place up to the present day.

Eventually the German tribes united to become England. The first Saxon king of England was Alfred the Great (871–899), though the first to really justify the title was his grandson Aethelstan (925–940). In the thirty-eight years following Aethelstan's death there were no fewer than five kings. This was interpreted as a sign of weakness by those who wished to claim power for themselves and when Aethelred II (978–1016) succeeded to the title at the age of ten he was the pawn in a ruthless power struggle.

The Danes invaded in 1013 and in the following year Aethelred II sought to divide and separate the Danish army on either bank of the Thames by pulling down London Bridge. This act gave birth to the still-popular nursery rhyme 'London Bridge is Falling Down'.

London Bridge was the only bridge connecting the old Roman city with the settlement of Southwark, an area later noted for its inns, among them the Tabard, the scene of the meeting of the pilgrims in Chaucer's *Canterbury Tales*. Not being a part of the City, the puritanical City authorities had no sway in Southwark and it became the entertainment centre for London, a riotous and rumbustious red-light district. Roger Tyrrell, in his contribution 'The London of Shakespeare and Dickens', cleverly explores the history of this area, always managing to connect it with William Shakespeare and Charles Dickens, both of whom knew it well.

From 1042 until 1066 England was ruled by Edward the Confessor ('Confessor' being a stage *en route* for sainthood). He moved his court from the City of London to Westminster. In so doing he set in motion a sequence of events which led to the location of Britain's legal heartland, the Temple, and to

many of the legal traditions still practised today. Legal
London is the subject of Richard Gadd's extraordinarily
detailed and entertaining contribution to this book, a chapter
which alone would demonstrate the erudition of City Walks'
guides.

Edward the Confessor's death left several contenders for the
throne, but succession passed to his strong and able
brother-in-law Harold Godwinson. The other contenders did
not take the succession kindly. The Norwegian king, Harald
Hardrada, invaded Britain in September 1066, but was
soundly defeated at Stamford Bridge in Yorkshire. Harold
Godwinson then marched south to meet the forces of William
of Normandy near Hastings. Harold might have won this
engagement, but a volley of arrows unleashed in his direction
by the Normans brought such hopes to an end – Harold was
killed, traditionally by an arrow in the eye. Strangely enough,
some 600 years earlier many Britons had fled to Brittany –
Little Britain – to escape the Saxon invaders. It is said that
their descendants joined William's invasion in 1066. The
native Britons had returned to claim their birthright, so to
speak.

Although there are some passing references to Jews in
Britain prior to 1066, it is with the Norman Conquest that
Jewish communities really began to proliferate in this
country. The growth of these communities is the subject of
another contribution by Roger Tyrrell, whose profound
knowledge of this surprisingly (to me) interesting subject
could and should fill a book.

During the late nineteenth century the East End of London
became the centre of settlement for immigrant Jews fleeing
Eastern Europe. In 1888 they became the subject of international attention as a result of a series of gruesome murders
committed by Jack the Ripper. The Ripper murders focused
attention on the terrible conditions in which the people of
Whitechapel lived and this resulted in the establishment of
many charitable institutions, some of which still function
today.

Jack the Ripper plays a not insignificant role in the history of the East End of London, not merely because of the social reforms which in part resulted from his crimes having focused attention on the area, but also because the concentration of media attention during the months when the murders took place has provided us with a singular piece of documented social history. Indeed, the media interest itself was largely due to increased literacy among the population and the corresponding growth of newspapers which catered for the newly literate. These papers specialized in reporting the sensational, such as great crimes and trials, and for such papers the Ripper murders were a gift which they capitalized on in their circulation wars.

But today the story of Jack the Ripper is for most people a 'who-dunnit' − was he a member of the Royal Family, an eminent doctor, the barrister Montague Druitt . . .? Over 100 years of speculation has led to many errors and a multitude of fantasies. An examination of some of these flights of fancy is the subject of the contribution to this book by Martin Fido, a trailblazer in the comparatively new study of crime history and one of the world's leading authorities on Jack the Ripper, being the author of *The Crimes, Detection and Death of Jack the Ripper*.

The final contribution is by Roger Tyrrell. It is an exciting, blow by blow account of the Blitz in World War Two and I think an appropriate conclusion to this book. We began with the Roman conquest and followed a series of invasions − each of which to some degree changed the face of London − concluding with the Norman Conquest of 1066. This was the last occasion that Britain was successfully invaded. The Blitz was the last time anyone attempted to invade Britain.

The six chapters in this book explore London on several levels. Each looks at a specific part of London, St Paul's, Southwark, Whitechapel, but each has an essential theme, religion, entertainment, crime. Encapsulated in one book, therefore, is 2,000 years of history − the history of a people and how they lived. But this book is more than that. It is a tour through that history as it can still be seen on the streets of London.

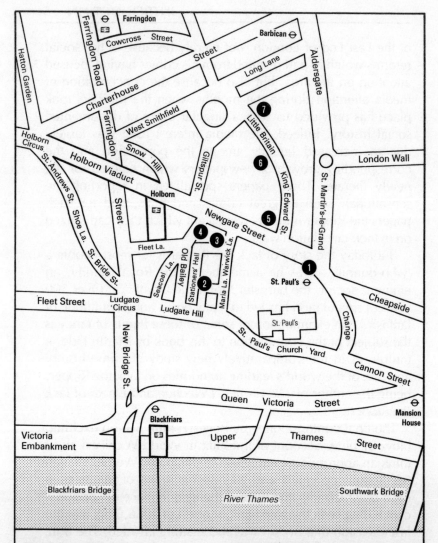

The Secret City

1 Panyer Alley. Immediately to your left as you leave St Paul's underground station is a short flight of steps. Set into the wall is a monumental stone dating from 1688, and below it is an inscription which takes us back to the origins of London.

2 Stationers' Hall. Until 1911 the Guild of Stationers controlled the publication of books and many authors found it expedient to become members.

3 Cutlers' Hall. The Guild Hall of the knife and fork makers.

4 The Old Bailey. Built on the site of Newgate Prison – possibly the most infamous prison in Britain – the Old Bailey has been the scene of some of the most celebrated criminal trials.

5 Christchurch, Newgate Street. Now war ruined, Christchurch was built on the site of the immense Greyfriars Monastery.

6 St Bartholomew's Hospital. London's oldest hospital.

7 The Church of St Bartholomew the Great. London's oldest parish church, it has a magnificent interior. Not to be missed.

THE SECRET CITY
Colin Oakes

The City of London hides its heart; behind a façade of glass offices and financial dealings, there is another city, a secret city of alleys, courtyards and a history of glamour and infamy. This aspect of the city is there for all to explore. Few penetrate its secrets, but those who do always come back for more.

Dominating the city is St Paul's Cathedral. It is the pivotal point from which to launch an examination of the surrounding area it has done so much to influence over the centuries.

There has been a *cathedra* or seat for the Bishop of London here since Anglo-Saxon times and the present cathedral is at least the fifth to be on the site. Tradition and occasional opportunities to examine the site archaeologically combine to suggest that there may have been a pagan temple preceding the Christian foundation. However, the full history of the site is unlikely to be known until the improbable opportunity to excavate under the building itself occurs.

Despite documents forged by the monks of nearby Westminster Abbey in an attempt to provide evidence that their foundation was of greater antiquity, it is generally agreed that St Paul's is older. According to the famous ecclesiastical historian Bede (673–735), St Paul's was founded in 604 and this date has been accepted by most historians.

The first cathedral was no doubt constructed of wood. Unusually it was not named 'London Cathedral' as is the case with, for example, Canterbury or Rochester. Instead its founder, St Ethelbert, King of Kent, gave it a personal name – 'St Paul's'. The first St Paul's burned down and was rebuilt in stone between 675 and 685 by Eorcanweald, fourth Bishop of London.

St Eorcanweald's tomb was associated with many miracles and during the medieval period it was an important site of pilgrimage, but his cathedral was destroyed by Vikings in 961. Their later presence was indicated by a gravestone in a distinctive style called Ringrike. It was found in St Paul's churchyard by Victorian workmen and depicts a stylized fighting dragon. The Viking runic inscription on the side indicates that it dates from the eleventh century, the time of King Canute (Cnut), famous in folklore for unsuccessfully ordering the tide to turn back.

The post-Viking cathedral, the third on the site, was destroyed by fire in 1087. By this time the Normans had conquered England and it may be that they privately greeted the loss with some satisfaction as it gave them the opportunity to rebuild St Paul's in their own style. The Norman cathedral was the wonder of the age. It was considerably larger and higher than the present St Paul's, possessing the tallest spire ever to have been built – it was 450 feet high! However, the reconstruction took so long that although it started out as a Norman Romanesque structure, it was completed in 1241 as a thoroughly Gothic building with massive flying buttresses and lancet windows. The cathedral was to be the focus of many processions, services of thanksgiving and ceremonies until its destruction, again by fire, in 1666. However, to the modern mind some of its uses would appear most strange.

Since the roads from Newgate and Ludgate went around St Paul's it was quicker to take a short cut through the cathedral to get to Cheapside. Horses would be trotted through the nave by their riders and this passing trade led to market stalls being set up along the length of the interior for the sale of all manner of goods. St Paul's was, therefore, a kind of medieval equivalent of a modern shopping mall. Archery, too, was practised inside the cathedral. Lawyers would meet clients there, and it was common for servants to be hired within its walls well into the reign of Queen Elizabeth I – in the second part of *Henry IV* Shakespeare has Falstaff say of Bardolph, 'I bought him in St Paul's'.

The fourth cathedral was repaired many times, most notably by the renowned architect Inigo Jones, but the fire damage of 1666 rendered it unsafe and it was finally demolished.

The present cathedral was designed and built by Christopher Wren, but he had to battle hard before the Church Commission would accept his 'modern' ideas. It took no less than three plans, each accompanied by much argument and compromise, before the Commission would permit the cathedral to be built with its 'popish' dome instead of the usual gothic spire. This apparently single dome is, as even a short tour within the cathedral will reveal, in fact a triple dome. The cathedral is also famed for the 'Whispering Gallery' with its fine acoustics, and the Stone Gallery with its excellent panoramic views over London.

On the interior dome are frescoes of stories from the life of St Paul. Whilst at work on them Sir James Thornhill is said to have stepped back to admire his work and came so close to the edge of the platform that his assistant was afraid to shout a warning in case Thornhill was startled into falling. With remarkable presence of mind, the assistant began to besmear some of the paintings, at which Thornhill angrily sprang forward – and was thus saved from almost certain death.

The crypt contains the tombs of Sir Christopher Wren (1632–1723), the Duke of Wellington and Admiral Lord Nelson. Nelson was interred in January 1806 having been brought back from Cape Trafalgar in a cask of brandy, allegedly less full on arrival than at the start of the voyage.

Because of its size and height St Paul's was very vulnerable to bombing during the Blitz (see Roger Tyrrell's chapter on London during the Blitz and the special measures taken to protect St Paul's). It was hit by incendiary bombs, but there was little major damage. Apart from relatively minor restoration and refurbishment as a consequence of war damage, the cathedral which greeted the Prince of Wales and Lady Diana Spencer on their wedding day in 1981 was essentially the cathedral as envisaged and built by Wren.

Wren began construction during the reign of Charles II and building continued during the reigns of James II, William and Mary, and was completed in the reign of Queen Anne. The completion and the Queen are commemorated by a marble statue standing in front of the cathedral. This is the second version of the statue, the first, erected in 1712, having deteriorated. The present copy by Richard Belt was erected in 1886. Although it portrays Queen Anne as relatively attractive, slim and cheerful, she was in reality ugly and fat. She also suffered the misery of seeing all her children die, none of them having exceeded the age of 14, and she had turned to drink. It was also unfortunate that her statue was sited not to face the cathedral, but instead to look down Ludgate Hill where in her day stood many brandy and gin shops. Children once cheerfully chanted:

Bandy Nan, Brandy Nan, you're left in the lurch,
Your face to the gin shop, your back to the church.

The antiquity and importance of St Paul's has meant that it dominated the surrounding district and this is most readily apparent in the religious names given to the roads in its neighbourhood – Ave Maria Lane, Creed Lane, Paternoster Row, Amen Court and Amen Corner. Actually there are no 'roads' in the City of London. For reasons not entirely clear all thoroughfares, alleys, etc., in the City itself are called court, lane, street, way, close – anything, in fact, but road. To return to the religious names, Paternoster Row (now a 1960s development) is linked to Newgate Street by Panyer Alley Steps.

Panyer Alley has no religious connotation; it derives from the panyers (bread baskets) which were made here for sale to the bakers of nearby Bread Street. However, the alley is interesting because of a monumental stone dating from 1688 situated on the south wall of the alley steps. It depicts a naked baker's boy sitting on his panyer and was re-erected in 1964 to commemorate the Panyer Boy, an ale-house which was destroyed in the Great Fire of London in 1666. It is the claim made in the inscription which is really the point of interest:

> When ye have sought the City round
> Yet still this is the highest ground.

These words are a reminder of London's antiquity and that the city was built by the Romans on the two hills of Ludgate and Cornhill: gravel hills rising out of the clay of the Thames's flood plain. It was long believed that Ludgate was the higher hill, but the wonders of modern surveying have proved this wrong. The eastern hill, Cornhill, is, in fact, about a foot higher than Ludgate!

Near Panyer Alley runs Ave Maria Lane. John Stow in his *Survey of London* (1604) says that it was so named because of the 'text writers and bead makers dwelling therein'. During the medieval period the street was part of a flourishing religious souvenir and book trade.

Also associated with religion, and later with commerce and government, the various guilds of the City of London, which were established from the twelfth century onwards, are to be found tucked away in the streets and alleys of the City. The guilds were created by craftsmen – barbers, butchers, blacksmiths, goldsmiths, brewers, etc. – to promote and protect their interests, both secular and religious and to ensure that their members received proper burials. The guilds are also known as the City Livery Companies because of the brightly coloured robes – their livery – that the members wear on ceremonial occasions.

One such guild headquarters is secreted in a courtyard off Warwick Lane – Stationers' Hall. The Brotherhood or Guild of Stationers, which until 1911 controlled the publication of books, dates back to the fifteenth century. Stationers' Hall itself dates from 1673, though the façade, by Robert Mylne, dates from 1800. The Hall was, regrettably, badly damaged by bombing in World War Two and restored between

1950-6. Many authors found it expedient to become members of the Stationers' Guild and these included Charles Dickens and George Bernard Shaw.

In Warwick Lane is the Cutlers' Hall. Despite their name, in medieval times the cutlers did not make cutlery, but simply fixed handles to knife blades. This is the Cutlers' fifth hall in a history dating back to the early fifteenth century. They moved here in the late nineteenth century and the building here today, despite damage in the Blitz, is the one erected in 1882. Their coat of arms displayed on the building has, unusually, a French motto instead of the more common Latin. The terracotta frieze on the façade, showing the process of cutlery manufacture, is by a Sheffield steelworker and primitive artist named Benjamin Creswick.

Before Cutlers' Hall was built this site was a meat market. The College of Physicians was also here from 1614 to 1825. It was here that William Harvey gave his lectures on the discovery of the circulation of the blood in 1674. More grimly, it was also at Physicians' Hall that dissections were performed for anatomical research and instruction. The Physicians had a supply of bodies of criminals executed at Tyburn public gallows and from Newgate Prison. Supplementing the supply were a group of thugs known as 'resurrectionists' or 'bodysnatchers' who dug up recently buried corpses and sold them to the surgeons for dissection. A fascinating book on this ghoulish subject has been written by Martin Fido, who has also contributed the chapter on Jack the Ripper in this book.

Not far from Physicians' Hall, on the site where the Old Bailey now stands, until 1901 stood the ancient and infamous Newgate Prison. This was the principal prison of the City of London authorities and had a reputation somewhat similar to that of the Bastille in Paris. Prisoners condemned to death were taken from Newgate Prison to Tyburn gallows – where Marble Arch (Speakers' Corner) now stands – and hanged. It has been estimated that between the twelfth century and 1783 about 60,000 people were executed there. Hanging days were public holidays and the roads leading to Tyburn were thronged with people come to see a 'hangman's jig' – an execution, so-called because the victims died from slow strangulation and frequently struggled for many minutes at the end of the rope. Some, surprisingly, survived the ordeal. In 1705, for example, a man named John Smith was restored to life after being suspended for the required time on 'Tyburn tree'. Learning nothing from his experience, he committed another crime shortly after and was again condemned to death but died in prison before he could dance his second 'jig'.

Not far from the Old Bailey, in Newgate Street stands the war-ruined Wren church of Christchurch. Christchurch was built on the ruins of the Greyfriars (Franciscan) Monastery of London. Built in 1225, the monastery occupied the entire area where the gardens and the ruined church now stand. In fact, Wren's church covers only the area occupied by the choir of this immense foundation. Greyfriars Passage marks the access to the church. After the Reformation the choir became a parish church with the King's Printer using the old nave as his workshop!

In 1553 King Edward VI founded an orphanage and school on the site of the monastery which became known as Christ's Hospital. Bequests to the orphanage were borrowed by the Mayor and Aldermen to finance the city. The inevitable problem was that, with the bequests tied up in numerous ventures, there was considerable trouble when the time came to pay the monies back to the orphans. The problem became so acute that at the end of the seventeenth century the City of London Corporation became temporarily bankrupt. The school continues to this day, now located at Horsham in Sussex. The students at the school still wear the uniform devised at the school's foundation, consisting of an ankle-length blue coat and yellow stockings in consequence of which the school is known as the 'Blue Coat School'; it was popularly believed that the yellow stockings deterred rats! Famous pupils at the school over the centuries include Samuel Taylor Coleridge, Charles Lamb and Leigh Hunt.

The Wren church on the site was gutted in the Blitz and

remains a ruin. Wren had built it with steep side galleries as a vantage point from which the masters could watch the pupils without them being aware of it. The steeple now houses an architect's office, and the shell of the church is a garden.

Leading off Newgate Street is King Edward Street. The name dates only from 1843 and commemorates King Edward VI, but it has had several other names during its long history. These include Blowbladder Street, Butchers Hall Lane, Chick Street and the notorious Stinking Lane. As may be imagined, it was a less than salubrious thoroughfare. This was the area of the 'Shambles', a street of slaughterhouses, and as far back as medieval times it was noted for the rank smell of rotting meat, bloated intestines and offal. The name of nearby Pig Lane came from an attempt to clean up 'Stinking Lane'. Pigs were kept there in the hope that they could be released into Stinking Lane to eat up the waste meat. It says much that the pigs, animals not generally noted as having gourmet palates, refused the meat and also refused to return to their sties. Instead they ran around the streets and even into people's houses.

Prior to the construction of the nearby British Telecom building, the site was excavated by archaeologists who found the remains of the church of St Nicholas in the Shambles. Many medieval skeletons were found and these have shed considerable light on our knowledge of the dietary habits, diseases and causes of death amongst medieval Londoners.

The butchers left the shambles site in the eighteenth century, but their presence here is commemorated by the Butchers' Hall of the Butchers' Guild in Bartholomew Close. Its location may raise an eyebrow or two − it is to be found surrounded by the buildings of St Bartholomew's Hospital!

As the religious street names owe their origin to St Paul's, so the large number of wholesale butchers, tripe dressers and the like in this area owe their existence to nearby Smithfield Market. There are, in fact, two Smithfields in the City. East Smithfield is located just north and east of the Tower of London. Both derive their name from their locality outside the city walls. To the north there were hills down which rainwater would flow until blocked by the wall. This created marshy areas and in some places moors and even open stretches of water, hence names such as Moorfields and Moorgate, and 'smoothfield', of which Smithfield is a corruption. 'Smoothfield' itself was so-named because the land was too wet for trees to grow and was therefore smooth. Near the centre of Smithfield some elm trees did grow. They were used for hanging criminals: in the medieval period Smithfield was the traditional place of execution, later replaced by Tyburn. The bodies were left to hang for two days and two nights as a deterrent to others. Probably the most famous person to be executed here was Sir William Wallace, the Scots patriot, who suffered this penalty for opposing the English invasion of his country in 1305.

During the later medieval period many people were burned at the stake here or, less commonly, boiled alive (giving rise to the nickname William Boilman for the Public Executioner). Boiling to death was only on the Statute Books for a little over a decade and was the prescribed punishment for poisoners. It was a treat for victim and spectators alike if the water was boiling before the prisoner was lowered in, otherwise it could take hours before death ensued. It was probably not with regard to the suffering of the victim that the water was brought up to the required heat, but to pacify the crowd of onlookers who were otherwise likely to become unruly through boredom while watching the prolonged suffering.

Burning at the stake could be as emotionally painful to the spectators as it was physically for the victim, as the process could be slow and protracted and the agonies of the victim readily apparent. Among the ideas put forward to shorten the process was one of placing a small barrel of gunpowder on a cord around the victim's neck. The resulting explosion not only limited the agonies of death but produced a spectacular conclusion to the entertainment for the audience.

Burning was usually a punishment reserved for heretics and those guilty of treason. Witches, who were frequently burned in Europe, were generally hanged in England. It would therefore produce a quicker, less agonizing death to profess allegiance to the Devil than to worship God in a manner not approved by the prevalent religious dogma of the day. Heretics could save themselves if they recanted before the flames consumed them, for the fire would then be extinguished. But there are several cases, such as an incident in 1410, where the victim reneged on his recantation after the flames had been put out. With extreme ill-will the executioner would pile up fresh wood and relight the fire.

Burnings became common during the Tudor period. After the Reformation only effigies of Catholics were burnt, but these had kittens inside them and the screams of the poor creatures, supposed to represent the screams of the Pope, were greeted with tremendous cheers from the assembled crowd of devout Protestants.

With the succession of Edward VI live Catholics were substituted for the kittens, and burning began in earnest. It is probable that had he not died young, Edward would today have a reputation equal to that of his sister, Mary I, popularly known as 'Bloody Mary'. Attempting to restore England to the bosom of the Catholic Church, Mary burned Protestants on a wholesale basis if they would not renounce their faith. On the south-east corner of the square in Smithfield is a plaque commemorating three of the more famous Protestants burnt here during Mary's reign. They include John Rogers, a translator of the Bible into English and originator of chapter and verse numbering in the work.

As well as executions, other entertainments were on offer for Londoners in this medieval 'Circus Maximus', such as jousts, tournaments and all sorts of games. There was even a popular revolt here – the Peasants' Revolt of 1381. Men from Essex, Kent and elsewhere in the southern counties, marched on London and the Tower to protest against, amongst other oppressions, the newly devised Poll Tax of the Chancellor, Simon of Sudbury. Having beheaded Simon on Tower Hill, the peasants were persuaded to camp a mile outside the City to the east at Mile End. The King, young Richard II, then agreed to negotiate with the peasants' leader, Wat Tyler from Kent, and guaranteed him safe conduct to a parley at Smithfield. As Tyler rode up to meet the King, the Lord

Mayor, William Walworth, later claiming that Tyler had threatened or abused the King, drew his dagger and stabbed Tyler who was then dragged off to nearby St Bartholomew's church and beheaded on a makeshift block. The King then proclaimed himself as the peasants' leader and persuaded them to disperse on the basis of promises he did not keep. Soon afterwards the other peasants' leader, Jack Straw from Essex, was beheaded at Smithfield. The only beneficiary of the affair seems to have been Mayor Walworth, a notorious brothel-keeper, who was knighted by the King for his services.

In the south-east corner of West Smithfield stands the gatehouse to the church of St Bartholomew the Great. The gatehouse is, to all intents and purposes, a modern fake simulating the nature of the old entrance. Parts of the stone gate date from 1240, but the rest dates from the restoration work undertaken in 1932. However, Tudor work does survive in parts, as the frame above is one of the earliest surviving timber frame house fronts in London. It was built in 1595 by William Scudamore, a parishioner of the church. He utilized recycled timbers, including a piece of a wooden rood screen from a church in London, which it is thought likely to have been St Bartholomew's itself. The present windows and the arrangement of the timber-framing date from the restoration of 1916 after a Zeppelin bomb damaged Scudamore's original.

The south-west doorway of the monastery hospital of St Bartholomew stood where this gatehouse stands today and to walk through it would have given access directly into the nave of the monastery church. In the days of heretic incineration in Smithfield the gateway would have provided a fine view of the ordeal for the assembled dignitaries such as the Lord Mayor and even royalty. In March 1849, during excavations for a new sewer just opposite this gateway, a mass of stones blackened by fire, ashes and charred human bones were found as mute testimony to this most dreadful punishment.

The church of St Bartholomew the Great beyond the gatehouse is London's oldest parish church and is a surviving fragment of an Augustinian priory founded in AD 1123.

Legend has it that it was founded by Henry I's court jester, Rahere, as thanks to God and St Bartholomew for delivering him from death from malaria contracted while in Rome. Rahere certainly became the first prior of the monastery but it was said he was not too proud to juggle at the annual fair held outside the church. There are, however, reasons for thinking that Rahere was not a jester but a priest in holy orders at St Paul's. Rahere, who died in 1143, was buried in the church and his tomb can still be found in the north-east corner. It is a very good sixteenth century copy of the original and portrays Rahere in the robes of a prior with his hands clasped and looking up to God; its simplicity saved it from iconoclastic destruction in 1642. However, in June 1866 the tomb was opened at the back, the bones uncovered and a piece of one of Rahere's sandals and a portion of his coffin were stolen. Even though these relics were recovered some twenty-four years later, the ghost of Rahere is said to hop around the church searching for his missing sandal!

The monastery at its greatest extent possessed a church measuring 300 feet by 86 feet from the gateway to the Lady Chapel. The existing church has the choir, Lady Chapel, transepts and crossing of the original and many features of note. Few of the surrounding monastic buildings survive, but of the cloister's thirty-six bays, three remain, coming off the church to the south with the chapter house door in the fabric. The door to the cloisters dates from the fifteenth century and only recently has it been placed back in its original position. The surviving parts of the crossing, where the nave and choir met, indicate the former presence of a huge central tower with turrets on either side. Documents claim the tower was struck by lightning in 1264. Repaired, it remained intact until a serious earthquake in 1382. The bell tower was rebuilt in 1405–9 and at the time of the Reformation had eleven bells; remarkably, the church still has five pre-Reformation bells today, more than any other church in England. The transepts have suffered the ravages of time and are much restored; however, the simple font in the south transept dates from the early fifteenth century, one of only two of this date in a London church.

The choir stalls are situated where they would have been in the thirteenth century. Here, in May 1230, Archbishop Boniface pronounced excommunications on the Bishop of London and the Dean of St Paul's. He then turned his attention to the prior who, however, was absent. The sub-prior now attracted Boniface's anger by remonstrating with him. Boniface, in heavy armour, rushed at the sub-prior, striking blows at his face and tearing his cope. He pinned the poor man to the choir stalls and crushed his lungs in the process. The sub-prior was carried to the infirmary while Boniface proceeded to excommunicate the prior, sub-prior, sacristan, cellarer and precentors of the priory. These sentences were shortly afterwards annulled by Pope Innocent IV.

In the choir, too, there was a monument which in the eighteenth century attracted much attention by weeping: however, the introduction of radiators in the twentieth century has eradicated the condensation which caused the miraculous phenomenon! On the other side of the choir from Rahere's tomb can be seen, up high, a projecting window or oriel built into the original round-topped Romanesque arch. This was built in 1515 by Prior Bolton. Beneath the window glass is his rebus which spells his name by images: a bolt going through a barrel or tun – bolt-ton.

The Lady Chapel has been much restored, but is a twelfth-century example rebuilt in the fifteenth century. It still has, high up, the niches for saints' statues, removed during the Reformation. These include the central space for Our Lady, the Virgin Mary. Below the chapel is a crypt, with a bone chute from above enabling the despatch of monks' bodies directly to their resting place.

When the priory was surrendered to Henry VIII on 25 October 1539, a sudden transformation overtook it. The nave was knocked down and the stone sold; a new west front was built and the monastery choir became a parish church. Uses for some of the buildings were bizarre. The cloister became stables, the north transept a cottage, the Lady Chapel three cottages and later still a printing office where Benjamin Franklin worked in 1725.

The hospital attached to the priory was secularized and continues to this day as St Bartholomew's Hospital, the oldest hospital in England in terms of its foundation. Although its parent priory had been dissolved, from 1544 the City Corporation administered it, passing control later to a Board of Governors. Nowadays it is a National Health Service hospital with a fine reputation for teaching and research. Popularly known as Bart's, it is one of the largest hospitals in London.

An annual fair was held from the year of the founding of the monastery until 1855. This was the famous Bartholomew Fair. Held on the open ground now covered by the square, Bartholomew Fair was a horse fair, but in the little street named Cloth Fair running alongside the church there was, as the name suggests, a fair for English broadcloth. It had been established by the monks to obtain revenue for their priory, every stallholder having to pay a rental to the monastery. The revenues of this fair, the largest in London, changed hands several times before the Reformation, during which time the reputation of the area declined. The nature of the market is well demonstrated by Ben Jonson's play *Bartholomew Fair*, with strolling players, wrestlers, dwarfs, fire eaters and tightrope walkers. However, the fair also attracted criminals – cut-purses who cut money from the purse at a victim's belt without the loser feeling the touch:

My masters and friends and people draw near
And look to your purses for that I do say,
And though little money in them you do bear,
It cost more to gain them to lose in a day.

Youth, youth they hadst better starve by thy nurse,
Than to live to be hung for cutting a purse.

Until Elizabeth I's time this was England's main cloth fair. Merchants came from all over Europe and the street itself was generally inhabited by drapers and cloth merchants, Inigo Jones's father among them. Although the inhabitants would have been troubled by the fair only on the three days a year it was held, the eve, day and morrow of St Bartholomew's feast day, there were many who were understandably against it and it is surprising it was not suppressed by the puritans in the seventeenth century. In 1688, at the traditional opening of the fair by the Lord Mayor, a tragic accident occurred. The Mayor, Sir John Shorter, whilst imbibing a 'cool tankard of wine, nutmeg and sugar' at the entrance of Cloth Fair, slapped the lid of the tankard down so loudly that his horse shied and threw him; he died the next day.

Gradually the City authorities saw the Fair as encouraging public disorder, and having bought the rights to it in 1830 from Lord Kennington, they suppressed it in 1855. Nothing now remains of the buildings in this street which survived the Great Fire of 1666, except the house at No. 41. The building is much restored and is all that remains of the three-storeyed longstyle houserow which was constructed in 1598. The remaining fabric largely dates from the seventeenth century. Next door to No. 41, in the alley, is a blue plaque marking the house in which Sir John Betjeman, Poet Laureate, lived until 1971. It is now Betjeman's Wine Bar and Restaurant.

North of the hospital and the square, the whole area is dominated by Smithfield Wholesale Meat Market. Covering an area of about ten acres, it is London's largest meat market. Trading in sheep, pigs, cattle and poultry has been conducted here since 1173. Although the City Corporation was granted the tolls on the market by Charter as early as 1400, it was not until 1638 that it was formally established as a market-place. As the growth of the city encroached upon the pens of the livestock market and slaughterhouses, the inadequacies of the site became increasingly apparent: there were no proper facilities for slaughtering and the blood flowed through the streets, the entrails being often simply dumped in the drainage channels. The average weekly sale had mounted by 1850 to 3,000 live head of cattle and 30,000 sheep: it was inevitable that something would have to be done. In 1855 the sale of livestock was transferred to the new Metropolitan Cattle Market in Islington and a new market building for meat was built on the Smithfield site by Horace Jones between 1851–66. Jones's plan was based on the design of the Great

Exhibition building, the Crystal Palace, with direct access to the market building by mainline railway. Although extensions have been constructed and the poultry section rebuilt after a fire in 1958, the present market basically remains the Jones design. There have been numerous suggestions for preparing the market for the twenty-first century by rationalization, but all ideas have met with opposition from the market traders and it is not clear at present in what form Smithfield will survive into the future. However, the market, with its sawdust-covered floors, cast and wrought-iron construction, its own police force and public house (licensed from 6.30am), allows a glimpse of the Victorian past.

Beyond the market buildings, in leafy Charterhouse Square, stands Thomas Sutton's Hospital in the Charterhouse. Originally a burial ground given to the city in 1350 by Sir Walter de Manny, the land, covering thirteen acres, was used as a mass burial pit for victims of the Black Death. The dead here, according to some estimates, number nearly 50,000. Twenty years later de Manny founded a Carthusian monastery on the site and this became known as the Charterhouse, a corruption of Chartreuse (after the parent house of the order). The original inhabitants were eight monks who lived in two-roomed cells and by 1398 there were nineteen such cells. It was an austere order; the monks lived in unbroken silence (as they still do today at the Carthusian monastery of La Trappe in Belgium), abstaining from meat and supporting themselves by their own labours. The only time they would eat together was on Sundays and Feast Days when they went to the refectory. After eating they could talk to each other during a three-hour walk outside the monastery, but even this was stopped during the period of St Bartholomew's Fair to prevent temptation.

Although the order was attractive to some – such as Thomas More who joined them for four years – their numbers were never great. The foundation nevertheless grew with fine, rich buildings and it was to be expected that they would come to the attention of Secretary of State Thomas Cromwell when the Act of Supremacy was passed in 1534. That year Prior John Houghton and two other Carthusian priors invited

Cromwell to the London Charterhouse to discuss the King's supremacy in church matters. As a result the Carthusians were sent to the Tower as rebels. On 4 May 1535, they were drawn on hurdles to Tyburn where they were hanged, drawn and quartered. Prior Houghton's arm was nailed to the gatehouse of the Priory as a warning to others and Cromwell's agents were placed in the monastery to report on the monks. In 1537 twenty monks signed the Oath of Allegiance required in the Act of Supremacy, ten others refused and were sent to Newgate and chained upright to the walls where nine of them died of starvation. The survivor was executed three years later at the Tower. A compliant prior, William Trafford, was appointed by Cromwell in 1537 and he surrendered the monastery to the king, who used it for storing tents.

In 1545 the Charterhouse became a private house. At first it was owned by Sir Edward North, who often entertained Queen Elizabeth here, then it passed to Thomas Howard, Duke of Norfolk who was executed in 1572 for plotting to marry Mary Queen of Scots. In 1611 the executors of Thomas Sutton bought Charterhouse in pursuance of his Will and founded a school for forty-four poor boys and a hospital for eighty poor gentlemen. Sutton's estate was not lacking in funds; on his death he was reputed to be the richest commoner in England, and aside from a few paltry bequests to various relatives and retainers, he had reserved the bulk of his funds for the project at Charterhouse. He was the model for Ben Jonson's great miser, Volpone. The school remained on the Charterhouse site until 1872 when it moved to Godalming in Surrey. Famous Carthusian scholars include John Wesley (founder of the Methodist Church), William Thackeray, Addison and Steele the journalists, Sir William Blackstone the jurisprudent, and Lord Liverpool, prime minister. Many of the buildings were damaged by an air raid in 1941, but plenty of the medieval, Tudor and later fabric still exists. Since 1949 the great cloister area has been used by St Bartholomew's Hospital as their medical school, but they in turn are shortly to vacate the site covering the old plague pit and the square in which football was first played in England. The pensioners remain, they are known as brethren and must be bachelors aged over sixty, of reduced means and practising members of the Church of England.

Neighbouring St John Street is named after the Priory of the Knights of St John of Jerusalem, the first centre in England for the order of Knights Hospitallers who were founded in AD 1100. The knights took religious vows and devoted them-selves to military service against the Saracens. They swore vows of poverty, chastity and obedience in much the same way as other monks, but were also active soldiers in the cause of the Crusades. Provision was made in their priory for the sick and the infirm, but the priory was not a hospital, it was a hospice or house of refuge. Any stranger could claim a share of the house for three days. This followed the rule of all monastic houses in Europe. The closeness of the priory to London brought many guests here, earning their keep of bread, beef and beer by bringing news from whence they came.

The buildings of St John's Priory once covered five acres, running from the end of St John's Lane down to Farringdon Street, which was then the course of the River Fleet. In the sixteenth century the monastery must have presented a grand sight. The gateway covered with lead sheeting led to three gardens where there was an orchard and a fishpond. The monastic complex consisted of the sub-prior's lodgings with gardens, the *turcopolier's* house and garden, the great and little courts, woodhouse and yard, plumber's house, laundry and counting houses. William Camden (1551–1623) de-scribes the priory very favourably:

> [It] resembled a palace, had a very faire church, and a toure steeple raised to a great height with so fine workmanship that it was a singular beauty and ornament in the City.

The monastery was suppressed by Henry VIII and its fine buildings became a kind of royal garden shed and store-house. In Henry's successor's time the buildings were blown up and the stones used to build Lord Protector Somerset's house on the Strand, leaving only the great gatehouse at the end of St John's Lane to remind us of its former glory.

This gatehouse was completed by Prior Docwra in 1504 and is a brick structure encased in stone typical of the Tudor period. It has been restored many times, notably by public subscription in 1845–6. One of its uses in Elizabethan times was as the office for the Master of the Revels, who granted licences permitting performances on the London stage. The leading dramatists came here, including William Shakespeare, thirty of whose plays were registered here. From 1731–81 the gatehouse was used as a printing works for Edward Cave's *Gentleman's Magazine*, to which Johnson, Garrick and Goldsmith contributed. Johnson even had a room here in which to write articles, poems and book reviews. Later, the gatehouse became the parish watchhouse, then a public house known as the Old Jerusalem Tavern, after which nearby Jerusalem Passage is named. Close by, Passing Alley has slightly less pleasant origins, having once been used by the desperate as an al fresco public convenience!

In 1874 the gatehouse was acquired by the order of the Hospital of St John of Jerusalem, a Protestant order established to uphold the traditions of the medieval Knights Hospitallers. From the room above the gate in 1874 was launched the famous St John's Ambulance Brigade. The gatehouse now contains the museum and library of the St John's Order, who care for and protect this remaining fragment of monastic London. Until quite recently, traffic still passed under the old gateway but this has now ceased and some measure of tranquillity has been brought to the spot.

The streets around St Paul's take us through all the ages of religious activity in London, from the pagan Romans to the present day, when the salvation of souls is probably of less immediate concern to the City than the *FT* or Dow Jones Indexes. Perhaps this is no bad thing; the pursuit of money may not be a virtue, but at least we don't burn stockbrokers at the stake for heretical dealings on the market!

The secret city hides its treasures well, but for those who pursue its long history an exciting voyage of discovery is to be enjoyed.

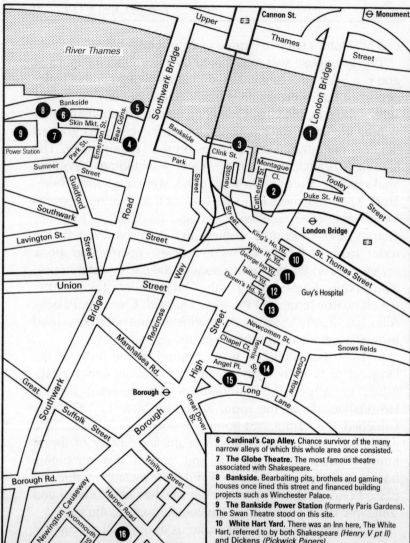

The London of Shakespeare and Dickens

1 London Bridge. The first river crossing here was built by the Romans.

2 Southwark Cathedral. An ancient pre-Conquest foundation.

3 Clink Street. A magnificent free-standing gable-end with rose window is all that remains of the banqueting hall of the Palace of Winchester. Clink Prison was also here.

4 Rose Alley. The Rose Theatre is located here.

5 The Anchor Tavern. Shakespeare may have lived in or near this spot.

6 Cardinal's Cap Alley. Chance survivor of the many narrow alleys of which this whole area once consisted.

7 The Globe Theatre. The most famous theatre associated with Shakespeare.

8 Bankside. Bearbaiting pits, brothels and gaming houses once lined this street and financed building projects such as Winchester Palace.

9 The Bankside Power Station (formerly Paris Gardens). The Swan Theatre stood on this site.

10 White Hart Yard. There was an Inn here, The White Hart, referred to by both Shakespeare *(Henry V pt II)* and Dickens *(Pickwick Papers)*.

11 George Inn Yard. Well worth a visit. The last remaining galleried coaching inn in the Greater London area. Referred to by Dickens in *Little Dorrit*.

12 Talbot Yard, The Tabard Inn. Chaucer's pilgrims met up here.

13 Queen's Head Yard. The sale of a pub here provided John Harvard with the money with which Harvard College was founded.

14 Tennis Street. Between Borough High Street and Tennis Street was the original King's Bench Prison.

15 Angel Place. The only surviving wall of the Marshalsea Prison where Dickens' father was imprisoned.

16 At the Horsemonger Lane Gaol, which stood on this site, appalling scenes at an execution caused Dickens to campaign against public hangings.

THE LONDON OF
SHAKESPEARE AND DICKENS
Roger Tyrrell

The Borough of Southwark, London's first suburb, lies immediately south of London Bridge. It developed as a result of the river crossing at the bridge. Over the centuries Southwark performed many functions for the city, but above all it was the entertainment district, the home of the great Elizabethan and Jacobean theatres – the Globe, the Rose, the Hope and the Swan. However, Southwark existed for many centuries before the arrival of the theatres.

The first London Bridge was built by the Romans, probably in about AD 100 and a little further down river from the present bridge. Archaeologists have discovered a massive timber structure on the north shore which is believed to be the Roman bridgehead. There was certainly a bridge here in the ninth century as the *Anglo-Saxon Chronicle* tells us of a woman accused of witchcraft who was thrown off it. During the first thousand years the bridges here were wooden structures which frequently collapsed or were destroyed in war. The most spectacular destruction of the bridge gave rise to the children's song 'London Bridge is Falling Down'.

In 1014 King Olaf of Norway, an ally of the English King Aethelred, who was besieged in the City of London, sailed his Viking longships up the river and tied ropes to the wooden bridge piers. Sailing back down river again, Olaf pulled the bridge and the Danish Viking army on it into the river. This feat was commemorated by the Icelandic poet Ottar Svarte in the thirteenth century *King Olaf's Saga*:

> London Bridge is broken down
> Gold is won and bright renown.
> Shields resounding
> War horns sounding
> Hildur shouting in the din
> Arrows singing
> Mail coats ringing
> Odin makes our Olaf win!

The first stone bridge was built here by Peter of Colechurch in 1176. By 1201, there are references to houses on the bridge; in the centre was a chapel dedicated to St Thomas à Becket. Becket, Archbishop of Canterbury, was murdered in his own cathedral in 1170, possibly at the instigation of King Henry II. Shortly afterwards Becket was canonized and became the first Londoner to achieve sainthood. The pilgrimage to his shrine at Canterbury was particularly popular with Londoners and began with prayers at his chapel on the bridge. At the southern end of the bridge was the gate (the 'Sutheringe Gewerke' in Old English) which gave its name to the suburb – Southwark. The gate was also used to display the heads of 'traitors', such as William Wallace, Jack Cade, Sir Thomas More and Bishop Fisher.

Between 1758–62 the houses were removed from the bridge and between 1823–31 a new bridge designed by Sir John Rennie was erected. Rennie's bridge was not particularly notable in architectural terms, being a simple five arch stone bridge. In the 1960s increased traffic flow had caused some subsidence of the bridge and it was decided to build a new and wider one. Rennie's bridge was sold to the McCullough Oil Corporation for £1,000,000 and transported to Lake Havasu City, Arizona, USA, in 1967–72. The present wider bridge was constructed around the old bridge in order not to interrupt the flow of traffic. Until 1760 the City

Corporation* had charged a toll to cross the bridge, which was paid into the Bridge House Estate Fund and used to maintain and repair the bridge. Although no monies have been paid into the Bridge House Fund since 1760, each successive version of the City's bridges (London Bridge, Tower Bridge, Southwark Bridge and Blackfriars Bridge) has been built free of charge on the public purse from the resources of the fund.

In *Oliver Twist* Dickens staged the meeting between Nancy, Mr Brownlow and Rose Maylie on the steps of London Bridge leading down to the river. These are the steps on the southern bank and the upriver side (the side closest to Southwark Cathedral):

> These stairs are part of the bridge; they consist of three flights. Just below the end of the second, going down, the stone wall on the left terminates in an ornamental pilaster facing towards the Thames. At this point the lower steps widen so that a person turning that angle of the wall is necessarily unseen by any others on the stairs who chance to be above him, if only by a step.

Noah Claypole, hiding on the steps at this point, overhears the whole conversation and his report of it leads to Nancy's murder by Bill Sikes.

When Rennie's bridge was transported to Arizona the southern shore arch was left behind on site thereby preserving the stairs which are nowadays known as 'Nancy's Steps'.

The traveller crossing London Bridge today leaves the City of London at the southern end of the bridge where heraldic griffins mark the boundary between the City and the London Borough of Southwark.

There are traces of Roman occupation on the riverside and the road leading south from London Bridge. *King's Olaf's Saga* refers to Southwark as a 'great cheaping town', in other words a great market place. In later centuries Southwark

---

* The City Corporation is the 'government' of the City of London covering only the original square mile — as opposed to the 680 square miles of Greater London. In this book 'City' (capital 'C') refers to the square mile.

would be the great hop market for the London breweries and
the Borough Market would become the third largest of
London's wholesale fruit and vegetable markets. From the
twelfth century onwards Southwark (the Liberties of Clink and
Bankside) was under the control of the Bishops of Winchester. Very early on, certainly by 1172, the Bishops operated
licensed brothels – known as the Stews of Southwark –
gaming houses and bear baiting pits all along the Bankside,
and these financed various enterprises such as Winchester
Cathedral. Eventually the Bankside would become the home
of the Elizabethan and Jacobean theatre. 'Bankside' refers to
the raised bank or levee along the riverside which protected
the low lying land here from flooding at high tide.

To the traveller crossing the bridge Southwark does not at
first appear an especially interesting place. One immediately
notes the shabbiness of the streets and many of the buildings
compared to the obvious opulence of the City on the north
bank. Yet there is much here to be discovered and to
fascinate the mind and eye of the careful and informed
observer.

Southwark's earliest development was along the river bank
and the road leading south towards Canterbury and Dover –
Borough Hill Street (Southwark is also known as 'The
Borough' since it was at one time the only borough in the
London area). Between St Thomas's Street and Borough
Underground Station, Borough High Street has dozens of
narrow lanes or 'yards' running off at right angles. They have
names such as White Hart Yard, Mermaid Yard, King's Head
Yard. This is because they were once the site of the great
coaching inns. Because of the houses on London Bridge, the
stage coaches and goods wagons could not cross the bridge
and so this street developed as the southern transport
terminus for London. Travellers would go to a specific inn to
travel to places in the south or to pick up goods or letters.

Charles Dickens knew six of the original stage coach pubs:

> There still remain [in Southwark] some half dozen old
> inns, which have preserved their external features

unchanged, and which have escaped alike the rage for public improvement, and the encroachments of private speculation. Great, rambling, queer, old places they are, with galleries, and passages, and staircases, wide enough and antiquated enough to furnish material for a hundred ghost stories. (*Pickwick Papers*)

Walking south, the first of these pubs of historic interest was the White Hart. All that remains in White Hart Yard to remind us of the past is a plaque on the wall telling us that the pub was 'immortalized by Shakespeare in *Henry VI* and by Dickens in the *Pickwick Papers*'. Shakespeare refers to the White Hart as the rebel leader Jack Cade's headquarters:

Hath my sword therefore broke through London Gates, That you should leave me at the White Hart in Southwark?

(*Henry VI* Part Two)

Dickens set a scene in the White Hart in Chapter Ten of *Pickwick Papers* – this is where Mr Pickwick and Sam Weller meet for the first time. Sam is working here as a bootblack cleaning the shoes of the customers and Pickwick is so impressed with Sam's cockney wit and wisdom that he decides to employ him as paid travelling companion in the adventures of the Pickwick Club. When Pickwick returns to his lodgings in Goswell Road in the City he asks his landlady, Mrs Bardell, if she thinks that 'two can live as cheap as one'. It is Mrs Bardell's mistaken interpretation of this question as a proposal of marriage that leads to the great legal action 'Pickwick v Bardell' for breach of promise.

The White Hart, in existence in 1406, was rebuilt in 1669 and thoughtlessly demolished by the railway company in 1889.

A little further on stands the George Inn, the last surviving galleried coaching inn in the Greater London area. There was an inn here in 1542 and probably before that. The present building dates from 1676, but in all likelihood closely resembles its predecessor. The range of buildings now here was matched by a similar structure opposite, with stables at the end of the yard. These, too, were unfortunately demolished by the railway company in 1889.

The structure of these coaching pubs may well have given rise to the standard layout of the Elizabethan theatres; in the days before the permanent public theatres were built, groups of strolling players would perform in market places and inn yards such as these. The inn yards were perfect for the actors' purposes; they could build a temporary stage, in front of which the audience could sit or stand, and in the galleries on either side of the yard, there was a ready made audience – the customers in the pub. The landlord did not pay the actors who took up a collection among the crowd, and the plays attracted extra customers for the pub. There is no documentary evidence that plays were ever presented in this yard in Shakespeare's day, but it is probable that they were.

Dickens refers to the George in *Little Dorrit*, though this is only a one line reference: 'if he goes into the George and posts a letter'. However there is an abiding memory of Dickens displayed in the bar. The story goes that Dickens was drinking here and ran out of cash. He borrowed from the landlord on the strength of his life insurance policy, but never returned to redeem it. His policy is still on display in the bar, showing Dickens to have been insured for one thousand pounds with the Sun Insurance Company.

The George is now the property of the National Trust and is a protected national monument.

Further on from the George stands Talbot Yard, a very unprepossessing alley leading to the back of Guy's Hospital. It is all that reminds us today of the Tabard Inn, the pub in which the pilgrims to Canterbury met up in Geoffrey Chaucer's *Canterbury Tales*:

> In Southwerk at the Tabard as I lay,
> Ready to wende on my pilgrimage
> To Caunterbury with ful devout corage
> At night was come into that hostelrye

Wel nyne and twenty in a companye,
Of sondry folk, by aventure yfalle
In felawshipe, and pilgrims were they alle,
That toward Caunterbury wolden ryde.
The chambres and the stables weren wyde,
And wel we weren esed atte beste.

The tavern Chaucer knew burned down in the great fire in
Southwark in 1676. It was rebuilt, but the landlord renamed it
the Talbot. A later landlord hung a notice at the entrance
announcing 'This is the Inn where Sir Jeffry Chaucer and the
nine and twenty pilgrims lay, in the journey to Canterbury,
anno 1383.' The Talbot was demolished in 1873.

Queen's Head Yard retains a few cobbles and great granite
blocks set at the width of a wagon's axles. This is all that
commemorates another of these vanished inns. This pub was
owned by the mother of John Harvard, who was born in
Southwark in December 1607. John's mother died in 1637
and he sold the pub, emigrating to Massachussetts Bay
Colony, where he died the following year. John left six
hundred pounds in his will for the foundation of a university
college. The governors of the colony put up a further five
hundred pounds and Harvard College was founded. There is
a memorial chapel in Southwark Cathedral for Harvard and a
local library named after him.

Continuing south, the signboard of the Blue Eyed Maid
appears – a rather primitive copy of a section of Botticelli's
Birth of Venus. There is a brief reference to this pub in *Little
Dorrit* – Arthur Clenam puts up for the night here on his return
to England. When Dickens, aged eleven, came up to London
from Rochester, he was sent up on 'Mr Simpson's Blue Eyed
Maid', a stage coach which took its name from the
destination pub. Hence, he may well have disembarked in
London for the first time here.

Further along Borough High Street stands the church of St
George the Martyr which also features in *Little Dorrit*, but the
careful traveller will find other Dickensian connections just
before he reaches the church. Just on the left, after the John

Harvard Library and running by the side of it, is Angel Place. In the preface to *Little Dorrit* Dickens tells us he had received many letters from readers during the serialization of the novel enquiring about the Marshalsea Prison and that to satisfy their curiosity and his own he went back there:

> Whosoever goes into Marshalsea Place, turning out of Angel Court, leading to Bermondsey, will find his feet on the very paving stones of the extinct Marshalsea jail; will see its narrow yard to the right and to the left, very little altered if at all, except that the walls were lowered when the place got free; will look upon the rooms in which the debtors lived; will stand among the crowding ghosts of many miserable years.

Even today the wall still stands, though the other buildings have gone. It is very atmospheric, particularly when viewed from the little garden on the other side of the wall off Tabard Street on a dark and wet day. The name of this prison derived from the Marshal of the King's Household. The exact date of its foundation is unknown but in 1381 it was attacked by Wat Tyler's rebels. Originally standing near Mermaid Court, it was rebuilt on the present site in the late eighteenth century.

Dickens's familiarity with this prison arises from the fact that his father, John Dickens, was imprisoned here for civil debt in 1824, when Charles was twelve years old. John Dickens was, amongst other things, a model for Mr Micawber in *David Copperfield* – a lifelong financial incompetent and bankrupt, hopeless at ordering his own affairs, but energetic and efficient with those of others. John was employed as a clerk in the Navy Pay Office and had been working at Portsmouth Navy Dockyard when Charles was born in 1812. When Charles was aged four and John was transferred to Chatham Dockyard on the River Medway in Kent, the family went to live in Rochester and here Charles passed the happiest years of his early life. Tragedy struck when John was transferred to the Admiralty in London. His salary could not keep pace with the expenditure of his London lifestyle and he was arrested as a civil debtor.

John was accompanied to the Marshalsea prison by Charles

who tells us in an autobiographical fragment that John's last words as he entered the gate were that the 'sun had set on him forever'. Charles continues:

> My father was waiting for me in the lodge, and we went up to his room (on the top storey but one), and cried very much. And he told me that if a man had twenty pounds a year, and spent nineteen pounds nineteen shillings and sixpence, he would be happy; but that a shilling spent the other way would make him wretched.

Desperate to prevent her husband being declared an insolvent debtor and, as a consequence, dismissed by the navy, Charles's mother, Elizabeth Dickens, attempted to organize a girls' boarding school, 'Mrs Dickens Establishment'. This was not an inspired idea. Elizabeth had no experience as a teacher and therefore no reputation. Further, it required the renting of large premises (at 4 Gower Street North, Bloomsbury) at a time when the family needed every penny it had. Charles later told his biographer, John Forster, that he spent a week posting leaflets through letterboxes in Bloomsbury announcing the opening of the school. But, he said, 'Nobody ever came to the school, nor do I recollect that anybody ever proposed to come, or that the least preparation was made to receive anybody.'

With the failure of the girls' school Elizabeth Dickens and all the younger Dickens children moved into the Marshalsea to be with John Dickens. Charles took lodgings in nearby Lant Street (just past Borough Underground Station) and each evening had supper with the family in the prison. He was sent to work at Warrens Blacking Factory where black polish was made. The factory stood where Charing Cross Railway Station now stands on the Strand, near Trafalgar Square. Charles's work here was pasting labels on jars of boot polish, supervised by another boy called Bob Fagin. The blacking factory reappears as the bottle washing plant of Murdstone and Grinby in *David Copperfield*, and Bob Fagin also had his rather unfair reincarnation in print. Here is Dickens's description of the prison in *Little Dorrit*:

Thirty years ago there stood, a few doors short of the church of St George, in the Borough of Southwark, on the left hand side of the way going southward, the Marshalsea Prison. It had stood there for many years before and it remained there some years afterwards, but it is gone now and the world is none the worse without it. It was an oblong pile of barrack building, partitioned into squalid houses standing back to back, so that there were no back rooms; environed by a narrow paved yard, hemmed in by high walls duly spiked at top. Itself a close and confined prison for debtors it contained within it a much closer and confined gaol for smugglers. Offenders against the revenue laws, and defaulters to excise and customs, who had incurred fines which they were unable to pay, were supposed to be incarcerated behind an iron-plated door, closing up a second prison, consisting of a strong cell or two, and a blind alley some yard and a half wide, which formed the mysterious termination of the very limited skittleground in which the Marshalsea debtors bowled down their troubles. Supposed to be incarcerated there, because the time had rather outgrown the strong cells and the blind alley, in practice they had come to be considered a little too bad, though in theory they were quite as good as ever. Hence the smugglers habitually consorted with the debtors (who received them with open arms), except at certain constitutional moments when somebody came from some office, to go through some form of overlooking something, which neither he nor anybody else knew anything about.

Next door to the Marshalsea stood (and still stands) the church of St George the Martyr, Borough High Street. Little Dorrit, who was born in the Marshalsea Prison, having visited Arthur Clenam one night, finds on her return that she is locked out and so, for the first time, spends a night outside the walls of the gaol. Eventually she is taken into the vestry of the church and given a church register to use as a pillow. The church is ultimately the scene of her marriage to Arthur Clenam.

The church was founded in 1122 and rebuilt by John Price in 1736. A stained glass window at the east end shows Little Dorrit wearing a poke bonnet.

Dickens's lodgings at Lant Street appear in *Pickwick Papers* as the lodgings of Bob Sawyer, a medical student at Guy's Hospital and 'a carver of and cutter of live people's bodies'.

Dickens describes Lant Street in *Pickwick Papers*:

> There is a repose about Lant Street in the Borough, which sheds a gentle melancholy upon the soul. There is also a good many houses to let in the street, it is a bye street too, and its dullness is soothing. . . . In this happy retreat are colonized a few clear-starchers, a sprinkling of journeymen bookbinders, one or two prison agents for the Insolvent Court, several small housekeepers who are employed in the docks, a handful of mantua makers, and a seasoning of jobbing tailors. The majority of inhabitants either direct their energies to the letting of furnished apartments or devote themselves to the healthful pursuit of mangling. The chief features in the still life of the street are green shutters, lodging bills, brass door plates and bell handles; the principal specimens of animated nature, the pot boy, the muffin youth and the baked potato man. The population is migratory, usually disappearing on the verge of quarter day, and generally by night. His Majesty's revenues are seldom collected in this happy valley, the rents are dubious and the water communication is very frequently cut off.

Southwark was an area rich in prisons. Further south from the Marshalsea was Horsemonger Lane Gaol where Dickens saw the public execution of Mr and Mrs Manning in 1849. The appalling scenes at this execution prompted Dickens to campaign for executions to be conducted out of public sight within the walls of the gaol.

Back along the Borough High Street towards the riverside stood the King's Bench Prison. This prison occupied the site now forming the junction of Borough High Street and Borough Road. *Nicholas Nickleby* seeking out the home of Brays is directed to a 'row of mean and not overly cleanly houses situated within the "rules" of the Kings Bench Prison, and not many hundred paces distant from the Obelisk in St Georges Fields'. Dickens tells us the 'rules' 'were a certain liberty adjoining the prison, and comprising some dozen streets in which debtors who could raise money to pay large fees, from which their creditors did not derive any benefit, were permitted to reside.' In *David Copperfield* Mr Micawber is imprisoned here for debt and David comes to dine with him.

Back at the riverside by London Bridge stands Southwark Cathedral, one of the most attractive and tranquil of the London cathedrals. It began life in the uncertain centuries before the Norman Conquest as the Priory of St Mary Overie (St Mary over the river). Legend would have St Swithun as the founder; this cannot be confirmed but there was certainly a 'monasterium' here at the time of the Domesday survey. In 1106 a new church was founded as the Augustinian Priory of St Mary Overie; fragments of this church remain. At the Reformation and Dissolution of the Monasteries (1537–1539) the surrounding monastic buildings were demolished and the church became the parish church of St Saviour at Southwark. It is by this name that the building was known to both Shakespeare and Dickens.

Dickens refers to the church in 'City of London Churches', a chapter in *The Uncommercial Traveller*:

> I know the church of old Gower's tomb (he lies with his head upon his books) to be the church of St Saviour's, Southwark.

The memorial to John Gower (d. 1408) is in the north aisle of the cathedral. He is shown resting his head on his three works: *Vox Clamantis* (in Latin), *Speculum Meditantis* (in French) and *Confessio Amantis* (in Middle English). The plot of *Confessio Amantis* is identical to Shakespeare's *Pericles, Prince of Tyre* and Shakespeare acknowledges his borrowing by making Gower the chorus in the play:

> To sing a song that old was sung,
> From ashes ancient Gower is come,
> Assuming man's infirmities,
> To glad your ear, and please your eyes.

In the south aisle is a memorial erected in 1912 to William Shakespeare. The window above the memorial shows characters from the plays. Shakespeare, of course, is not buried here. This is simply a memorial to his association with the church and district. Indeed, had Shakespeare not had the very good sense to have written a four-line curse to be inscribed on his tomb in the church of the Holy Trinity at Stratford-upon-Avon, he would long ago have been dug up and reburied in Poets' Corner, Westminster Abbey, but so far no one has found the courage to defy the curse:

> Good Friend for Jesus sake forbear,
> To digg the dust enclosed heare.
> Blest be ye man yt spares thes stones,
> And curst be he yt moves my bones.

Set in the floor of the St Saviour choir are memorial stones for John Fletcher (collaborator with Shakespeare on *Two Noble Kinsmen* and co-author with Francis Beaumont of *The Knight of the Burning Pestle* and other works); Philip Massinger, author of *A New Way To Pay Old Debts*, *The City Madam* etc.; and Edmund Shakespeare, 'a player base born', who died in December 1607. Edmund, Shakespeare's brother and sixteen years his junior, probably died of bubonic plague. In all probability it was William who paid 'four pence for a toll of the great forenoon bell' at Edmund's funeral. That afternoon the players were probably back at work in the theatre.

In Shakespeare's day, Philip Henslowe, a local landowner,

theatre builder and impresario, and his son-in-law, Edward Alleyn, who was regarded as the finest of the Elizabethan actors, were the churchwardens here. Also in the south aisle is the monument to Launcelot Andrewes, Bishop of Winchester and chief translator of the English Bible in 1604 (The King James or Authorized Version).

In 1905 a diocese of Southwark was created and the church containing the *cathedra* of the Bishop of Southwark became Southwark Cathedral. It is a very active community church, and campaigns on many social issues, having a long association with the cause of ordination of women.

Walking west along the riverside from the Cathedral, one passes through streets of refurbished Victorian riverside warehouses and new office blocks extending the activities of the City of London across the river. The area covered today by Winchester Walk, Winchester Square and Clink Street was once the palace of the powerful Bishops of Winchester. In Clink Street, a free-standing gable-end with a rose window is all that remains of the great banqueting hall of the palace.

This area was known as the Liberties of Clink and Bankside. Medieval law was very uneven and was largely a matter for the feudal lord who ruled a particular district. It was in their capacity as secular lords that the bishops ruled Bankside and turned it into a medieval red-light district. This was in response to the City of London authorities across the river. Dominated by puritanical merchants, singing, dancing, prostitution, gambling, and finally the theatre had been banned in their area of jurisdiction. The bishops seized the commercial opportunity and transformed Bankside into the area of the 'stews' – the riverside brothels. The women who worked in them were known as 'Winchester Geese'. In back of the brothels there were gambling dens and bear and bull baiting pits, making the Southwark riverside a rumbustious but dangerous area.

The palace was originally built for William Giffard, Bishop of Winchester, in 1109. Henry VIII may have met his first wife, Catherine of Aragon, here. The last bishop to occupy the palace was Launcelot Andrewes (d. 1626). During the

English Civil War (1642–48) the palace was taken over by parliament for use as a prison for Royalist soldiers, and was later sold for warehousing. The palace was never actually demolished, but over the centuries slowly disappeared in redevelopment of the warehouses. The movement of shipping further downriver in the early 1970s led to the wholesale redevelopment of this area, thereby exposing the remains of the banqueting hall.

Being the landlords of so many houses of dubious virtue, the bishops found it necessary to run a prison for offenders against such law and order as they chose to impose. This was known as the Clink Prison and it stood by the riverside in the street now called Clink Street. It is not certain when the first prison appeared here, but it is first mentioned in 1509. In his *Survey of London*, John Stow says that it was kept for people who broke the peace in the Bankside brothels. However, it later housed poets, among them Thomas Dekker and Christopher Smart. Other celebrated inmates included Bishop Hooper and John Bradford, both burned at the stake in 1555.

Thomas Dekker was a contemporary of Shakespeare and collaborated with him on at least one play. His best known work is *The Shoemaker's Holiday*, which contains the lines:

> Golden slumbers kiss your eyes,
> Smiles awake you when you rise,
> Sleep, pretty wantons, do not cry,
> And I will sing a lullaby.

Dekker died in the prison of gaol fever (typhus).

Christopher (Kit) Smart (1722–71) also died in the Clink. His friend Dr Samuel Johnson, commented on Smart's confinement:

> ... he has partly as much exercise as he used to have, for he digs in the garden. Indeed before his confinement he used for exercise to walk to the ale-house; but was carried back again. I did not think he ought to be shut up. His infirmities were not noxious to society. He

insisted on people praying with him; and I'd lief as pray
with Kit Smart as anyone else. Another charge was that
he did not love clean linen; and I have no passion for
it . . .

Smart's best known poem 'Jubilate Agno' (1759–61)
contains a delightful section 'For I will consider my cat
Jeoffry':

> For I will consider my Cat Jeoffry.
> For he is the servant of the Living God duly and daily
> serving him . . .
> For first he looks upon his forearms to see if they are
> clean.
> For secondly he kicks up behind to clear away there.
> For thirdly he works it on stretch with the forepaws
> extended.
> For fourthly he sharpens his paws by wood.
> For fifthly he washes himself.
> For sixthly he rolls upon wash.
> For seventhly he fleas himself that he may not be
> interrupted on the beat.
> For eighthly he rubs himself against a post.
> For ninthly he looks up for his instructions.
> For tenthly he goes in quest for food.

Delightful though this poem is (and I have only quoted a
small part of Jeoffry's doings) it is easy to see how Smart may
have caused doubts about his sanity to arise in the minds of
his eighteenth-century contemporaries.

Further along the riverside from the Clink the area is known
as Bankside and would eventually become the home of the
Elizabethan and Jacobean theatre, although there was a
prelude to this on the other side of the river.

Until the Renaissance dramatic entertainment in Europe
largely consisted of religious plays, such as the medieval
mystery plays, and troupes of clowns, jugglers and dancers.
The mystery plays would be performed at fairs, in the market

places of towns or in the western porticoes of the churches. But with the revival of interest in classical civilizations there was also a revival of the Greek comedies and tragedies. Companies of strolling players were formed to present these plays and would wander from town to town, stopping to perform wherever they found a likely audience. The players could no longer use the church porticoes because the church deeply disapproved of the new entertainment, so they began to use the yards of inns such as those in the Borough High Street. These yards were ideal for their purposes with their galleries for spectators surrounding the open space of the yard where a temporary stage could be erected. It is more than probable that the structure of the inn yards influenced the design of the theatres when they finally emerged.

England's first theatre was built in 1576 by James Burbage. It was located in Shoreditch, just to the north of the city, and was quite simply called, 'Theatre'. It was used by the 'Earl of Leicester's Men' and later by the 'Lord Chamberlain's Men' – to avoid arrest as vagrants, all the Elizabethan companies acted under, and adopted the name of, royal and aristocratic patrons. The Burbage company's decision to build a fixed site theatre must indicate considerable experience as a company of strolling players – the company was confident that the audience would come to it, rather than the actors going in pursuit of the audience. It was in this theatre that William Shakespeare first performed as an actor and for which he wrote his first plays.

We do not know when or how Shakespeare entered the theatre, but he did so during the years 1585–92. Known as the 'lost years' because they are devoid of any documentary reference to him, they are, nevertheless, rich in speculation and legend.

One of the most abiding legends about Shakespeare was launched in 1709 by Nicholas Rowe. According to Rowe, Shakespeare was caught poaching deer in a private park called Charlecote Park, near his home in Stratford. Shakespeare went on the run as a fugitive from justice and ended up outside the 'Theatre' in London. This theory was elaborated by Robert Shiels in 1753 in his *Lives of the Poets of Great Britain and Ireland* (not the most truthful source, it was published under the name 'Mr Cibber', who had little or nothing to do with it):

> Concerning Shakespear's first appearance in the play-house. When he came to London he was without money and friends, and being a stranger he knew not whom to apply, nor by what means to support himself. At that time coaches not being in use, and as gentlemen were accustomed to ride to the playhouse, Shakespear, driven to the last necessity, went to the playhouse door, and pick'd up a little money by taking care of the gentle-men's horses who came to the play; he became eminent even in that profession, and was taken notice of for his diligence and skill in it; he had soon more business than he himself could manage, and at last hired boys under him, who were known by the name of Shakespear's boys: Some of the players accidentally conversing with him, found him so acute, recommended him to the house, in which he was first admitted in a very low station, but he did not long remain so, for he soon distinguished himself, if not as an extraordinary actor, at least as a fine writer.

This may well be, but it is equally possible that Shakespeare joined one of several companies of actors known to have performed in Stratford in these misty years and simply ended up in the 'Theatre' when the troupe returned to London.

The 'Theatre' remained in Shoreditch until 1598, and during this period the following plays by Shakespeare are recorded as having been censored or performed: *The Comedy of Errors*, *The Two Gentlemen of Verona*, *The Taming of the Shrew*, *Henry VI* Parts I, II and III, *Richard III*, *King John*, *Titus Andronicus*, *The Merchant of Venice*, *A Midsummer Night's Dream* and *The Merry Wives of Windsor*.

In 1598 a dispute arose between the Burbage company and the landlord, Giles Allen. Allen was attempting to increase the rent and take possession of the building after another five years. The company responded by dismantling the 'Theatre' and transporting its timbers across the river. Allen, in a deposition made to court, describes how the actors

riotously assemble[d] themselves together and then and there armed themselves with divers and many unlawful offensive weapons, as namely, swords, daggers, bills, axes, and such like, and so armed did then repair unto the said Theatre. And then and there, armed as aforesaid, in very riotous, outrageous, and forcible manner, and contrary to the laws of your Highness's realm, attempted to pull down the said Theatre, whereupon divers of your subjects, servants and farmers, then going about in peaceable manner to procure them to desist from that their unlawful enterprise, they, the said riotous persons aforesaid, notwithstanding procured then therein with great violence, not only then and there forcibly and riotously resisting your subjects, servants and farmers, but also then and there pulling, breaking, and throwing down the said Theatre in very outrageous, violent and riotous sort, to the great disturbance and terrifying not only of your subjects, said servants and farmers, but of diverse others of your Majesty's loving subjects there near inhabiting.

The theatre was carried across London Bridge by the 'rioters', who numbered among them William Shakespeare, and was rebuilt in Midden Lane (now Park Street), Bankside, and renamed the Globe. It was necessary now to give the theatre a more distinctive name since Phillip Henslowe, inspired by the success of the north bank theatre, had begun building theatres on the south bank.

The first of the south London theatres built in 1586–7 by Henslowe and John Cholmley was the Rose in Rose Alley, off modern Park Street. Edward Alleyn became the principal actor here and played the lead in the first performances of Marlowe's *Dr Faustus*, *Tamburlaine*, etc. Many of the works of Chapman, Chettle, Dekker, Drayton, Greene, Kyd and

Lodge were performed here too. Shakespeare's *Titus Andronicus* was first performed in the Rose by Lord Sussex's Men. This performance is particularly important since a sketch was made of the costumed players on stage. This is the only contemporary illustration we have of one of Shakespeare's plays in performance.

Many other companies performed at the Rose, which appears to have been a sort of repertory theatre, and these included the Lord Admiral's Men, Lord Strange's Men, the Lord Chamberlain's Men, the Earl of Pembroke's Men and the Earl of Worcester's Men.

In 1989, during redevelopment, archaeologists excavated the site, discovering the foundations and thereby much information on the structure of this and Elizabethan theatres in general. Sadly, the Secretary of State for the Environment, Nicholas Ridley, overruled the protests of Lord Olivier, Dustin Hoffman, the Royal Shakespeare Company and many others, deciding that the Rose was *not* an historic monument! A grotesque concrete office block is now rising over the site. Until recently the developers (Imry Merchant plc) actually had the effrontery to display a sign stating that they were 'preserving the Rose Theatre'; their 'preservation' apparently means that when this latest piece of barbarism reaches the end of its unedifying career, in sixty years or so, archaeologists will again have a chance for a glimpse of the Rose.

The Rose was followed in 1594 by the Swan, built by Francis Langley (whose name appears in a writ with William Shakespeare) and located in the Paris Garden (now the Bankside power station). The stage of this theatre was sketched in 1596 by Johannes de Witt, giving us our only visual representation of the Elizabethan stage (the sketch made at the Rose shows only the players and not the structure of the stage itself).

Disaster struck the Swan in the form of royal retribution in 1597. Langley had staged a play called *The Isle of Dogs* by Nashe, Chapman, Jonson and others; this play was denounced by the Privy Council as 'contanynge very seditious and slanderous matter'. The Privy Council immediately closed all playhouses and ordered their demolition. Fortunately the destruction was not carried out, but the Swan seems never to have recovered from the blow. The theatre declined and was occasionally used for fencing matches and prize fights until it was pulled down circa 1632.

It was at the Globe that Shakespeare would spend the rest of his career. The leading actor of the company (originally the Lord Chamberlain's Men, later [1603] the King's Men) was Richard Burbage. Other actors included Augustine Phillips, William Sly, John Heminges, Henry Condell, Cuthbert Burbage, Thomas Pope and William Kempe. Will Kempe was the great jester of the Burbage company, having pioneered the roles of Peter in *Romeo and Juliet* and Dogberry in *Much Ado About Nothing*, but in 1602 the restless and eccentric Kempe left the company to dance the Morris from London to Norwich. Having achieved this to his satisfaction, Kempe then danced over the Alps and out of the history of the Globe. He was replaced by Robert Armin, a much more subtle comic and tragedian than his predecessor. It was Armin who in 1605 first played the Fool in *King Lear* with Richard Burbage in the title role.

The Globe, in common with the other public theatres of the time, was a circular (in fact polygonal) structure, with three tiers of galleries surrounding an open inner circular space into which the stage projected. The audience could stand or sit in front of it. Above the stage was a turret containing pulleys and devices for swinging things or people onto the stage. There were also cannon balls to be rolled across the floor of the 'tiring house' for effects such as thunder, and stage cannons for the alarms of war. From the turret flew a flag with a globe upon it to announce a performance in progress, and a trumpeter would sound out from the turret to summon the crowds.

The Globe burned down on 29 June 1613, during the first night of Shakespeare's *Henry VIII*. There is a scene in *Henry VIII* that requires the firing of a stage cannon. This was done but it set fire to the thatched roof of the galleries. The whole theatre burned down. In a letter to his nephew, Sir Edmund

Bacon, Sir Henry Wotton described the event:

> The King's players had a new play, called 'All is True',
> representing some principal pieces from the reign of
> Henry VIII, which was set forth with many extraordinary
> circumstances of pomp and majesty, even to the matting
> of the stage, the Knights of the Order with their Georges
> and garters, the Guards with their embroidered coats,
> and the like: sufficient in truth within a while to make
> greatness very familiar, if not ridiculous. Now, King
> Henry making a masque at Cardinal Wolsey's house,
> and certain chambers being shot off at his entry, some of
> the paper, or other stuff, wherewith one of them was
> stopped, did light on the thatch, where being thought at
> first but an idle smoke, and their eyes more attentive to
> the show, it kindled inwardly, and ran round like a train,
> consuming within less than an hour the whole house to
> the very grounds.
>
> This was the fatal period of that virtuous fabric,
> wherein yet nothing did perish but wood and straw, and
> a few foresaken cloaks; only one man had his breeches
> set on fire, that would perhaps have broiled him, if he
> had not by benefit of a provident wit put it out with
> bottle ale.

The Globe was rebuilt and was open again by 1614, but
Shakespeare seems to have decided that this was the time to
retire. He went home to Stratford-upon-Avon, where he died
three years later in 1616. In *The Tempest*, written in either
late 1612 or early 1613, Shakespeare seems almost to have
anticipated the end of the Globe:

> Our revels now are ended. These our actors,
> As I foretold you, were all spirits and
> Are melted into air, into thin air:
> And like the baseless fabric of this vision,
> The cloud-capp'd towers, the gorgeous palaces,
> The solemn temples, the great globe itself,
> Yea all which it inherit, shall dissolve

And, like this insubstantial pageant faded,
Leave not a rack behind. We are such stuff
As dreams are made on, and our little life
Is rounded with a sleep.

(The Tempest)

The Globe continued with John Fletcher replacing Shakespeare as the playwright. But finally, along with the other theatres, it was suppressed by the Civil War Parliament of 1642 and pulled down.

On 12 October 1989, during redevelopment, archaeologists discovered what are believed to be the foundations of both Globe theatres. It was immediately announced by the property developers, Hanson Corporation, that they would restructure their development around the remains and that these will be preserved on site. They will go on display to the public when the building is completed in a year or two.

When the Globe burned down in 1613, Philip Henslowe and Jacob Meade seized the opportunity to poach the audience by building the Hope Playhouse on a former bear garden near the site of the Globe. This new theatre had a movable stage and could thus be used for bull and bear baiting spectacles as well as regular dramatic presentations. The background to this was that the City of London, having banned theatre but failed to prevent its development outside the area of its jurisdiction, had approached the government in the form of the Privy Council and appealed to them to ban the theatre altogether. They argued that there was a danger of infection in the playhouses: large numbers of people being gathered together increased the risk of bubonic plague, which had been endemic in London over several centuries. Accordingly the Privy Council forbade the presentation of plays in any week when the deaths from plague mounted above thirty in the City of London. This generally meant the summer. The players responded by taking to the road in summer as strolling players. This banning, incidentally, gives us our modern conception of the 'season' in the theatre. The plays would normally be presented in the spring and autumn.

In the winter the light was too poor and in any case, nobody wanted to stand still and watch a drama for an hour or two in winter weather.

However, Henslowe and his son-in-law, Edward Alleyn, had spotted a loophole in the law; it banned the plays, but said nothing about bull or bear baiting. In 1604 Alleyn had bought the title of Master of the Royal Bears, Bulls and Mastiff Dogs. Henslowe and Alleyn, therefore, used the Hope as a bear and bull baiting pit.

Baiting was a disgusting entertainment. It consisted (in the case of the bear) of chaining a European brown bear to a post and then setting six wild dogs loose. The audience would bet on how many dogs would be killed before they gave up attacking the bear. It was an extremely barbaric sport, but then England was an extremely barbaric country. Queen Elizabeth is known to have visited the bear baiting on at least nine occasions, once with the Spanish ambassador. King James was fond of this grotesque sport. There are some eighteen references to bear baiting in Shakespeare, and we can thus assume that he was familiar with, if not approving of, the 'sport'. Ben Jonson, who had become the resident playwright at this theatre cum bear-pit, in *Bartholomew Fair* has the Book-Holder mock the Stage Keeper for 'sweeping the stage and gathering up broken apples for the bears within.'

Oliver Cromwell suppressed bear baiting in the course of the English Civil War. Lord Macaulay, the nineteenth-century historian, rather unfairly said that Cromwell did not do this because 'of the pain it gave to the bears, but because of the pleasure it gave to the spectators.' But Cromwell was unsuccessful. In later years Samuel Pepys and his wife saw 'some good sport tossing of the dogs; one into the very boxes': John Evelyn however found it a 'rude and dirty pastime'. Not very far from here, in Southwark Bridge Road, are the National Headquarters of The League Against Cruel Sports. No longer, thankfully, campaigning against bear baiting, the League's activities are now largely directed against what Oscar Wilde described as the 'unspeakable in pursuit of the uneatable' – foxhunting.

The museum on the site of the Hope Playhouse is operated by the International Shakespeare Globe Trust which is currently building a replica of the Globe Playhouse on Emerson Street and Bankside. The museum consists of models of the Elizabethan theatre and displays documenting the players, playwrights and companies of the Bankside. Any profit from the entrance fees goes towards the building of the new Globe theatre.

Many people have questioned Shakespeare's existence and his authorship of the plays. Personally, I am totally convinced that Shakespeare was the author of the plays attributed to him. It appears to me that what feeds this speculation is a class-based inability to accept that someone from as lowly a background as Shakespeare's could possibly have made this magnificent contribution to literature. There is a whole industry nowadays dedicated to proving that William Shakespeare either did not exist, or, if he did, was not the author of the plays that bear his name.

Some believe that Shakespeare's plays were written by the Earl of Southampton, others that they were written by Edward de Vere, Earl of Oxford. A particularly strong and very vociferous group believe the author was Francis Bacon, Lord High Chancellor of England. There are quite serious groups of devotees convinced the author was Queen Elizabeth I! Yet others think the plays were written by a committee, and Calvin Hoffman, an American engineer, believes that Christopher Marlowe wrote them. There are a few problems with Hoffman's theory, as indeed there are with all the others. But the principal objection to Hoffman's case is that Christopher Marlowe was murdered in a pub brawl in Deptford in 1593. This has not deterred Hoffman, who believes that Marlowe survived and had a clandestine existence for the next twenty years or so, during which he paid the none-too-bright, bit-part actor William Shakespeare to put his name to Marlowe's plays. Well. . . .

There is no doubt that William Shakespeare existed. The documentary evidence for his life is overwhelming; indeed, given the period and his social class, we know a great deal more about Shakespeare than we might reasonably expect to do. The most convincing evidence, not only for Shakespeare's existence but for his authorship of the plays, comes from his contemporaries who, often hostile, are the least likely sources of mythology.

The first certain reference we have to Shakespeare amongst fellow literati comes in September 1592: Robert Greene, university wit, playwright, debauchee, and – when it comes to the likes of Shakespeare – snob, lay dying in a hovel with his common law wife, his bastard child and a massive grudge. Greene died of the rather unusual complaint of a 'surfeit of pickled herrings', but had time to write a last note to the world, 'The Repentance of Robert Greene, Master of Arts and Greene's Groatsworth of Wit, bought with a million of Repentance . . .'

> Base-minded men all three of you [probably a reference to Marlowe, Nashe and Peele], if by my misery you be not warned: for unto none of you (like me) sought those burrs to cleave: those puppets (I mean) that spake from our mouths, those antics garnished in our colours. Is it not strange, that I, to whom they all have been beholding; is it not like that you, to whom they all have been beholding, shall (were ye in that case as I am now) be both at once of them forsaken? Yes, trust them not: for there is an upstart crow, beautified with our feathers, that with his *tiger's heart wrapped in a player's hide* supposes he is as well able to bombast out a blank verse as the best of you; and, being an absolute Johannes Factotum, is in his conceit the only *Shake-scene* in a country.

Greene's reference to the 'tiger's heart' is clearly an allusion to Shakespeare's line in *Henry VI* Part Three in which the Duke of York, about to be slain, inveighs against Queen Margaret shouting: 'O tiger's heart wrapp'd in a woman's hide!'. Greene is evidently accusing Shakespeare of plagiarism, but at the same time is explicitly admitting to us that Shakespeare has written this play, borrowed plot or otherwise. Greene also helps us date this play as being written before September 1592.

Ben Jonson, though not as mean-minded as Robert Greene, was not the man to throw compliments around without due cause. In the Introduction to *Bartholomew Fair* he sideswipes at those 'that beget tales, tempests, and such like drolleries'. Shakespeare was godfather to one of Jonson's children, yet Jonson prided himself on his honesty:

> I remember, the players have often mentioned it as an honour to Shakespeare, that in his writing (whatsoever he penned) he never blotted out a line. My answer hath been, would he had blotted a thousand. . . .

Not kind, but explicitly recognizing Shakespeare's authorship, he continues:

> . . . for I loved the man, and do honour his memory (on this side of idolatry) as much as any. He was indeed honest, and of an open, and free nature, had an excellent phantasy, brave notions, and gentle expressions, wherein he flowed with that facility . . . he redeemed his vices with his virtues. There was more in him to be praised than pardoned.
> *Timber or, Discoveries Made upon Men and Matter*
> (1641)

The riverfront at the end of Bear Gardens is the stretch known as the Bankside and it was here that the stews once stood. Henry II in a letter to the Bishop of Winchester attempted to introduce some order into proceedings here. One of Henry's regulations allowed the brothels to paint signs on the front of the buildings as a form of advertising to the potential customers across the river. Each stewhouse had a name similar to those of taverns: the Falcon, the White Hind, etc. Of the houses, only one remains today: Cardinal's Wharf (No. 49 Bankside) is the former Cardinal's Cap brothel, although the present building probably dates from about 1700. The Cardinal's Cap was named after Cardinal John Beaufort (son of John of Gaunt) – the suggestion being that the cardinal's cap could be found inside the house.

There is a plaque on the side of the house which tells us Sir Christopher Wren lived here during the building of St Paul's Cathedral. This does not appear probable as the construction of St Paul's had been in hand at least twenty-five years before Cardinal's Wharf was built, and in any case Wren's addresses (Great Russell Street, Whitehall, etc.) are well known. The second half of the plaque contains the even less probable assertion that Catherine of Aragon landed here on her first arrival in England. The plaque was put up by Dr Axel Munthe, whose family still own the house.

Cardinal's Cap Alley, running by the side of the house, is a chance survival of the narrow alleyways which once covered the area. One can imagine the ease with which muggers once preyed on their victims in such places.

Next door to Cardinal's Wharf is the site of the new Globe theatre being built by the International Shakespeare Globe Trust (founded by Sam Wanamaker). The new Globe will, as far as fire regulations permit, be a replica of the original. The plans are based on extensive research and have been modified in accordance with information derived from archaeological excavations. It is hoped that the theatre, which will seat 900, will open in 1992.

Back downriver towards Southwark Bridge stands Bear Wharf, one of the old ferry points across the river. Until 1760 London Bridge was the only crossing over the river in the City area. Since a toll was payable on the bridge it was equally expedient to take a ferry. These operated from Bull Wharf on the northern shore to Bear Wharf. Note the stained glass window on Bear Wharf showing a bear in the baiting pit.

Dickens invariably refers to Southwark Bridge as the 'Iron Bridge'. The bridge Dickens knew was designed by Sir John Rennie and opened in 1819. It was on the Iron Bridge that John Chivery proposed to Little Dorrit. *Our Mutual Friend* opens with Gaffer and Lizzie Hexam rowing their skiff between Southwark and London Bridges fishing dead bodies out of the river – the gruesome means by which Gaffer earned his living.

Passing under Southwark Bridge, back towards London Bridge, the weary traveller will find a charming eighteenth-century pub, the Anchor, which may well stand on the site of a fifteenth-century one, the Castle on the Hoop. It is possible that Shakespeare lived in a house on or near this spot during his time in Southwark. In Dr Samuel Johnson's time the Anchor was owned by Mr Henry Thrale, also owner of the Southwark brewery which stood on the site of the Globe Theatre. The 'Globe' and 'Boswell' bars in the pub are named in memory of its connections. The brewery which once stood on the site of the Globe eventually became a massive Courage brewery and though this has long since moved out of town, the thirsty pilgrim can still drink a decent pint in one of the atmospheric bars.

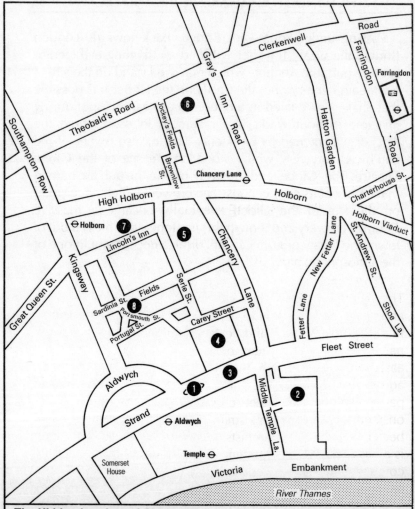

The Hidden Interiors of Old London

1 St Clement Danes. The original church survived the Great Fire of 1666, but was demolished in 1679 to be rebuilt by Wren.

2 The Temple. It takes its name from the English headquarters of the Knights Templar and New Temple, a round church built by the Knights.

3 Temple Bar. This monument, in the middle of the road, marks where The Strand becomes Fleet Street and takes us back to pre-1066 London.

4 The Law Courts. In 1190 this area was known as Fickett's Field. The Knights Templar used it as their military training ground.

5 Lincoln's Inn. Most likely named after Henry de Lacy, the third Earl of Lincoln; the alumni of this Inn included Oliver Cromwell, William Penn and Jeremy Bentham.

6 Gray's Inn. This Inn failed to impress Dickens, who said of it: '. . . one of the most depressing institutions in brick and mortar known to the children of men'.

7 The John Soane Museum. Not to be missed at any cost; among the delights to be found here are original works by Hogarth including the *Rake's Progress.*

8 Portsmouth Street. A remnant of rural London: two farm labourer's cottages dating from 1567, now called The Old Curiosity Shop, take us back to when this was an area of fields.

THE HIDDEN INTERIORS
OF OLD LONDON
Richard Gadd

The visitor to London, brought up in a town or city planned and designed according to some logical scheme, may at first find the apparent lack of order or planning in London's street pattern perplexing. Instead of being numbered and running east-west or north-south, the streets here have names, and to add to the confusion the name of a street will often change part way along. The streets curve, wind, nearly double back on themselves. London's street plan would appear to have been developed by anarchists, drunks or surrealists. Yet there is a logic behind the apparent disorder: it is an historical one covering nearly two thousand years of development and redevelopment.

The area we today call Greater London covers 680 square miles and is controlled by more than thirty local government authorities, but the original London was a minuscule area covering only one square mile. The City of London founded by the Romans in AD 43 was until 1760 surrounded by an imposing wall on three sides and by the River Thames on the fourth. Even today the City is an independent territory governing itself almost in isolation from national government. Beyond the walls of the city were villages and hamlets – Kensington, Chelsea, Bermondsey, Tower Hamlets, etc. – and these eventually grew to become the suburbs of the city itself. The fields between disappeared under a sea of brick and concrete. The winding roads and the innumerable 'High Streets' in London, are reminders of, on the one hand, the country lanes that connected the villages, and on the other, that each hamlet looked inward and so towards its own principal street.

To add to the confusion there is also the fact that Greater London contains within its area not one but two cities which developed quite independently of each other – the Cities of London and of Westminster. It is the district in which these two cities border each other that this chapter will examine, the district flanking the double-named street Strand/Fleet Street, the area of the Inns of Court, the Royal Courts of Justice, of the Temple, Lincoln's Inn and Lincoln's Inn Fields.

In 1060 King Edward the Confessor moved his residence from the ancient City of London westward along the riverbank to a location next to a monastic settlement that would eventually become Westminster Abbey. This was to have a profound effect on the development of London, separating the City of London, which would continue to develop as a commercial and financial centre, from the City of Westminster, which would become the seat of royal and later parliamentary government.

In Edward's day the City was connected to Westminster by a sandy bridle path along the north bank of the Thames. This path was later replaced by a road which in Westminster was called the Strand (as in beach) and in the City was called Fleet Street (after the River Fleet which flowed at its eastern end). At a point on the road that was originally unoccupied land a chain had been stretched as one of the outer defences of the City of London. This place was described in 1301 as 'a void place extra Barram Novi Templi' (outside Temple Bar). Temple Bar derived its name from the Knights Templar who in 1162 had founded their English headquarters about halfway along this road. By 1351 the chain had been replaced by a permanent gateway with a prison above it and was now the administrative boundary of the two cities.

In those days merchants, noblemen and the general populace still lived largely within the walls of the City and

The 'Panyer Boy' in Panyer Alley,
near St Paul's.

The George Inn off Borough High
Street.

The remains of the Banqueting
Hall of the Bishop of Winchester's
Palace, Clink Street.

Prince Henry's Room, Fleet Street.

The Cock Tavern (1549), Fleet Street.

Mary Kelly's room, Miller's Court, off Dorset Street, Spitalfields.

Buck's Row (now Durward Street). Scene of the first Ripper murder.

there were open fields between the City and Westminster. By the time of Queen Elizabeth I the noblemen, in order to be closer to the royal court, had built houses along the riverbank south of the Strand. In 1666 the Great Fire of London destroyed some nine-tenths of the City and now many wealthy men and aristocrats took the opportunity to settle outside of the City itself. They built in the area north of the Strand, the part of Westminster known today as the West End. Here they created spacious and well ordered squares in deliberate contrast to the narrow, treeless streets and winding alleyways of the older City. The latter part of the seventeenth century saw intense speculative development, and stylish Palladian townhouses were built, in marked contrast to the less sophisticated pomp of the merchants' houses and the public buildings of the City.

Each city represented a different ethos; one a city of aristocratic fops seeking preference at court as a means of supporting their elegant but vacuous lifestyles, the other a city of Puritans, Presbyterians and Calvinists ruthlessly dedicated to the pursuit of profit through shipping, insurance, financial speculation and general trade. The City merchants deeply disapproved of the fripperies of the West End with its expense on fine clothing, carriages, the theatre, literature and art. In turn the West End found the moneymakers boorish.

During the rebuilding of the City after the Great Fire Christopher Wren had emerged as the most eminent architect of his day and was commissioned to design a new gateway at Temple Bar in a more fitting style for the pretensions of the City of London. By the mid-nineteenth century Wren's Temple Bar had become an obstruction to traffic on the Strand and Fleet Street ('a bone in the throat of Fleet Street'). It was dismantled in 1877–78. A proposal to remove it had been advanced more than a century before. The horror generated among the burgers of the City is well expressed by a certain Anthony Pasquin, who in 1788 warned in his 'The Metropolitan Prophecy':

> If that gate is pulled down, twixt the court and the City,
> You'll blend in one man, prudent, worthless and witty.

If you league cit and lordling as brother and brother,
You'll break order's chain, and they'll war with each other.
Like the Great Wall of China, it keeps out the Tartars
From making irruptions where industry barters.
Like Samson's wild foxes, they'll fire your old houses,
And madden your spinsters, and cousin your spouses.
They'll destroy in one sweep both the mart and the forum,
Which your fathers held dear, and their fathers before
them.

A memorial to Temple Bar was erected in 1880 (the work of Horace Jones) and it marks the point where Fleet Street becomes the Strand. The gate itself was re-erected on a private estate at Theobalds Park, Hertfordshire, and is now in a very poor state of preservation. One plan for its future is to incorporate it as part of the Paternoster Square redevelopment near St Paul's.

The gateway owed its name to New Temple, a round church built nearby by the Knights Templar, a powerful religious order who called it New Temple to distinguish it from their earlier church built in what is now High Holborn. The Temple lies to the south of the Bar and is now an area of squares and gardens, quiet and reclusive with an academic air. Accessible from Fleet Street by one of two narrow lanes, this enclave houses the Honourable Societies of Middle Temple and Inner Temple. These are two of London's four Inns of Court – the legal district. Under a mile to the north is Gray's Inn, connected to the Temple by Chancery Lane, and between the two, with a gateway in Chancery Lane, is Lincoln's Inn. How lawyers came to be conveniently located between Westminster and the City is a fascinating story which starts with crusading chivalry and ends in corruption.

The story begins in 1118, when a French knight, Hugue de Payans, founded the crusading order of the 'Poor Knights of Christ of the Temple of Solomon in Jerusalem', or put more simply, the Knights Templar. The Templars were founded to protect pilgrims travelling to holy places in Jerusalem and to crusade against the 'infidel'. Their ruthless dedication to this cause made the order extremely rich and influential. Ten years after the foundation of the order a branch had been established in England and Scotland. Their first head-quarters was in Holborn, but in about 1162 they moved to the north bank of the Thames around Fleet Street. An area known as Fickett's Field was acquired, *circa* 1190, as their military training ground; it occupied the area where the Royal Courts of Justice now stand on the Strand.

The Templars trained hard. They saw themselves as the élite of Christendom, and although they had taken vows of poverty and chastity they were often far from monk-like in behaviour. Their order held interests in properties, farms, breweries, mills, churches and chapels in hundreds of places from Cornwall to the North Riding of Yorkshire. Fired by the conviction of their own superiority they had little sympathy for the plight of others. Only the Pope had control of their actions, they were beyond the reach of secular law. Richard I granted them a Charter of Liberties in 1189 that exempted the Templars from many taxes. These 'property-less' monks acquired wealth and luxury by any means, including where necessary arson and murder.

The Paris Temple became the centre of European finance, and France was to be the scene of the Templars' fall and destruction. The King of France, Philip le Bel, convinced that God was acting through him, desired to be a Roman emperor, ruling from Jerusalem over a federation of nations. Two things stood in his way, the bankruptcy of his realm, and the power of the Templars. However, in 1305, L'Esquiu de Floyran gave the king an account of the secret rituals of the Templars.

As part of the initiation ceremony the young monk would be taken behind the altar, where he would spit on the crucifix and kiss the base of the spine of the Master of the Order (or vice-versa). The Templars were also accused of regularly indulging in sodomy. None of these accusations were true; the Templars were ruthless men, but they were not blasphemers or sodomites. However, confessions were extracted under torture and then pressure was brought to bear on the Pope. In 1308 Pope Clement V dissolved the order and Philip razed the Paris Temple to the ground, seizing its treasures and burning the Master, Jacques de Molay, at the stake on the Île de France.

In England in 1324 Edward II assigned the Templars' lands to the Knights Hospitallers of St John and they in turn leased it to lawyers. The exact date that lawyers took up residence in the New Temple is not known, the records having been destroyed in the Peasants' Revolt of 1381. The oldest record of Middle Temple dates from 1501, and that of Inner Temple from 1505. However, sometime after 1324, the Temple became, in effect, a medieval university of law.

The Inns were so called because they were hostels (in Latin, *hospitium*) housing students as well as being places of instruction for law apprentices. Originally there were more than four Inns of Court, one of the earliest being Clifford's Inn, located on the north side of Fleet Street. Dating from 1345, it was rebuilt at various times, ceased to be an Inn of Court or Chancery at the end of the nineteenth century, was the residence of Virginia and Leonard Woolf in 1912–13, and was almost completely demolished in 1934.

Originally, advocates were drawn from the ranks of the clergy; ecclesiastics then being the only educated class. The students, who led a celibate life and attended church services under compulsion, served a seven year apprenticeship under a master. During this time they would attend meetings, called moots, and readings conducted by advanced students, utter barristers, given the title of Reader, where points of law would be debated. The Honourable Societies were, and still are, governed by Benchers, senior lawyers, who alone have the power to call students to the Bar. Readers from the Bench would advance to Serjeant at Law and reside in Serjeant's Inn on Chancery Lane before becoming judges. Each year two Readers would be elected.

Moots, mock trials, of the Honourable Society of Middle Temple were held in Middle Temple Hall. The present hall dates from 1570–74 and was built by Edmund Plowden, the then Treasurer of Middle Temple. To say Plowden built the hall is to say he raised the money to build it. This he obtained by fining lawyers who refused the office of Reader (senior barrister). This was a medieval university tradition. On being promoted the student would be expected to entertain his fraternity by holding a lavish banquet. These were very expensive, although the Inns had by Plowden's day become finishing schools for the gentry, and were not only teaching law but also music, history and dancing. Some students were unable to bear the expense of a banquet and instead paid a lesser amount as a fine. This was not good for their career prospects but ensured that only those students financially capable of holding high office, with income from their estates, ever got to do so. Later, a mandate of King James I denied admission to the Inns of Court to anyone who was not a gentleman by descent.

During the seventeenth century the readings system fell into decline, and it was only necessary to eat meals in hall to establish residence. (The system was revived in 1852 with the establishment of the Council of Legal Education). Today students must sit exams set by the Bar Council, but much of the tradition remains. A successful candidate cannot practise law at the Bar without first obtaining a pupillage in one of the Inns. He will carry a lawyer's books around for him, do some of his research and after about two years might take on his first brief. With this apprenticeship served he can now earn money, but only if he has eaten twenty-four times in his hall. Any barrister must eat three times each law term in his hall if his membership of his society is not to lapse.

Middle Temple Hall is not generally open to the public. This is a pity since within there is a magnificent oak double hammer-beam roof with an Elizabethan carved oak screen which served as a backdrop for the first performance of Shakespeare's *Twelfth Night* on 2 January 1601 in the presence of Queen Elizabeth herself. The high table at the western end is a single plank of oak twenty-nine feet long, a gift from Queen Elizabeth I to the society. Close by is another smaller table called the Cupboard, a gift from Sir Francis Drake, who was a member of Middle Temple. The coats of arms of hundreds of Readers from over the centuries cover the wooden panelled walls and are also displayed in stained glass in the windows.

Above the entrance of the hall can be seen an emblem of the Knights Templar, the Lamb of God carrying the Flag of Innocence, which the Middle Temple has adopted as its emblem. The gate has a Tudor Rose, i.e., the white rose of York superimposed on the red rose of Lancaster, symbolizing the re-unification of the country under the Tudors after the Wars of the Roses between the Houses of York and Lancaster (1455–85). Indeed, according to Shakespeare the argument that led to the wars began in old Middle Temple Hall and continued in Middle Temple Gardens with the antagonists picking roses as a symbol of their dispute.

Within the precincts of the Inns the church of the Knights Templar still stands today. Architecturally it is an unusual building, using both Norman and Gothic styles. The old western main door is a richly decorated Romanesque arch, now sadly deteriorating: the portal is Gothic. The nave of the church is round, in common with all Templar churches, and modelled on the Dome of the Rock in Jerusalem where they had their original headquarters. Heraclius the Patriarch of Jerusalem consecrated the church in 1185, dedicating it to St Mary. The rectangular choir to the east is an extension built in 1220–40, and access to the church is by the door on the south side of the choir.

The nave interior shows the same mix of styles: a Norman triforium supported on Gothic arches with piers of Purbeck marble (not a true marble but a sedimentary rock with a high fossil content enabling it to take a high polish) – the first use of this stone in London. Carved heads decorate the capitals of the pillars in the round nave. Interestingly, the church has some of the best post-World War Two stained glass in London, namely the east window (1957–8) by Carl Edwards.

On the floor lie life-sized effigies of knights – not Templars, since most of them died and were buried in the Holy Land –

but rich patrons of the order, who in return for giving generously to the cause would not spend too much time in Purgatory. The crossed legs of an effigy signify that the knight had been on a crusade, or that he would have liked to have gone to the Holy Land.

One of these knights was Geoffrey de Mandeville, who was killed by an arrow in the forehead when attacking North-ampton in 1144. Being a kindred spirit and patron, the Templars wished to bury him in the Old Temple Church, but as he had been excommunicated for sacking Bursar Abbey and killing the monks he could not be buried in consecrated ground. Instead, his body was encased in a lead coffin and suspended from a branch of a tree overhanging the chur-chyard. Thus he was as close to consecrated ground as possible without actually being in it. He was later pardoned.

Plowden died in 1584 and is buried in the church. He was a Catholic which at that time could have been dangerous. Henry VIII had broken from Rome over the Pope's refusal to grant him a divorce from Catherine of Aragon. He needed an heir, Catherine had not successfully produced one, but Anne Boleyn might if he could marry her. So he passed a series of Acts to make the divorce from Catherine possible. Among these a 1540 Act abolishing the Hospitallers, resulted in the Temple Church changing from a Papal Peculiar to a Royal Peculiar, which means today that the Sovereign, with the Archbishop of Canterbury, appoints the clergyman and not the Bishop of London.

The Master of the Temple in 1540, William Ermestede, showed what had to be done to keep a position. He had been ordained a Catholic priest (and subject to the Pope through the sub-prior of the Hospitallers) and Henry allowed him to stay in office. He then became a Protestant chaplain to Edward VI, a Catholic again in Mary's reign, then a Protestant chaplain to Elizabeth I. He died a Protestant in 1559. Plowden had more conviction. He defended a man accused of attending mass, and in the course of the trial elicited that the mass had been conducted by a layman, not a priest. He therefore argued that if there was no priest there could have been no mass. His client was acquitted.

Close to the south door is a glass panel set in the floor and lying beneath is the gravestone of John Selden. He went to Oxford University but failed to graduate, became a student at Clifford's Inn, was admitted to Inner Temple in 1604 and called to the bar in 1612. Living in the period in which the Long Parliament would overcome Charles I, execute him, and establish a short lived republic, he was at heart a sceptic and unwilling to support either Parliament or the King. His career as a lawyer was erratic; he was fined in 1624 for refusing to be a Reader yet in 1633 he became a Bencher. He thought that there was an ordered liberty to be found in the ancient pre-Norman constitution of the country and so in his political career he was consulted by commoners on their rights and by aristocrats on their privileges. But as England prepared itself for civil war, he said, 'If men would say they took up arms for anything but religion, they might be beaten out of it by reason; out of that they never can for they will not believe what you say.' It is ironic that he lies in the Temple Church, a church founded by religious fanatics.

Opposite the church is Inner Temple Hall. Dating from 1955, it replaces a nineteenth-century Gothic structure destroyed in the Second World War. It is not an interesting building, but the Inner Temple emblem, the winged horse Pegasus, can be seen on the rain water downpipes. This was adopted as an emblem during the Christmas revels held in honour of Lord Robert Dudley in 1563. The original Templar symbol, a horse with two riders, was mistakenly recarved by a stonemason as Pegasus. The riders portrayed were Hugue de Payans and another knight and they were so poor they had to share horses − and that is more incredible than a real winged horse would be!

Mrs Thatcher, had she pursued her career in the law instead of switching to politics, would have taken her meals, and felt quite at home, in this neo-Georgian hall. But in common with about sixty per cent of all successful Bar Council examinees, and those not obtaining a pupillage, she changed course.

Inner Temple Lane is flanked by two rather drab buildings dating from 1857; Goldsmith Building and Dr Johnson's Building. Goldsmith, author of *The Vicar of Wakefield* and the comedy *She Stoops to Conquer*, spent much of his life in the Temple evading creditors, having a weakness for expensive clothes and reckless generosity. Johnson lived in chambers at 1 Inner Temple Lane. He said of his friend Goldsmith, 'No man was more foolish when he had not a pen in his hand, or more wise when he had.'

Johnson, by living among lawyers, was familiar with the legal and political issues of the day. A Tory with Jacobite sympathies, he supported the Stuart claim to the throne over that of the occupying Hanoverians. Others did not share his opinion. But George III, perhaps the first of the modern kings, was seen by many to be the apolitical foundation of everything that was worth defending in the British State and the ultimate safeguard for English liberty. Johnson was a 'friend to subordination', it being 'most conducive to the happiness of society. There is a reciprocal pleasure in governing and being governed.' His biographer, Boswell, wrote: 'He talked in his usual style with a rough contempt of popular liberty ... Political liberty is good only so far as it produces private liberty.' The expression of English freedom in the eighteenth century could be found on the street outside his chambers. It was not to be found in the lawyers' commentaries or their legal niceties but with the Englishmen who believed that they, and not merely their superiors, were freeborn. Imitating and often mocking the pretensions of their social superiors, they presented an unexpected sight to an observer like Voltaire. Visiting England in 1728 he was surprised to learn he had been watching ordinary men and women, apprentices and streetwalkers dressed up to imitate fashionable idlers.

Boswell appreciated this street life. He was fond of picking up streetwalkers and celebrating 'melting and transporting nights of love' with them. In his *Life of Johnson* he wrote: 'On the 9th of April [1772] ... He [Johnson] carried me with him to the church of St Clement Danes, where he had his seat;

and his behaviour was, as I had imagined to myself, solemnly devout. I shall never forget the tremulous earnestness with which he pronounced the awful petition in the Litany ...'. While in church Boswell surprised himself by 'laying plans for having a woman' while experiencing the 'most sincere feelings of religion'.

Johnson's statue outside St Clement Danes faces along the Strand to Fleet Street, almost as much his spiritual home as the church.

St Clement Danes is the Central Church of the RAF. The wall of the church is pock-marked from shrapnel, a reminder of the Battle of Britain. St Clement is the patron saint of Denmark, but the association of the church with the Danes is not clear. It is possible that when Alfred the Great captured London, having laid siege to it *circa* 880, he drove most of the Danes off, but allowed those who had married Saxon women to remain in the environs of the church.

At about the start of the eleventh century the original wooden church was replaced by one in stone. This escaped destruction in the Great Fire of 1666 (which extended no further west than the Inner Temple), but by 1679 it was declared to be in such a poor state of repair as to be unsafe. All but the tower was demolished and a new church was built in its place. It was designed by Sir Christopher Wren, who managed to incorporate the old tower into the new building. He also provided the church with an apse, a singular feature in a Wren church which is shared only by St Paul's. The church is actually *not* pure Wren: the Wren building was not considered grand enough for its location and in 1719 James Gibbs raised the tower by twenty-five feet and added a fifty-foot baroque steeple.

Although the Great Fire failed to claim St Clement Danes, the church did not escape the bombing in World War Two. Hit in December 1941, the exterior remained largely intact, but the interior was gutted and restoration was not completed until 1958. Inlaid in the floor are over 750 badges in Welsh slate of the various squadrons and units of the RAF who fought in World War Two. Also to be seen are the Shrines of

Remembrance containing the names of men who died in action, some of whom were American airmen who died in Britain. The church has a sombre mood, appropriate to a war memorial, though not in keeping with Wren's light and spiritual design.

Outside the west door is a statue of Lord Dowding Commander-in-Chief of Fighter Command during the war. More than anyone, he knew that at the end of the Battle of Britain the RAF's forward stations could sustain themselves for little more than a week (see Roger Tyrrell's chapter on 'The City in the Blitz'). Their destruction would have made Hitler's Operation Sealion (the land invasion of Britain) possible. Dowding is credited with the invention of the 'operations room'.

Standing by Johnson's statue a fine view is to be had of a building which has been described as 'that Gothic pile which we can never wholly see, and in which Street [its architect] just failed to design a truly complete, effective, and absolute building, and failed entirely to produce a building practically suited for its purpose.' Just what is its purpose? Is this a medieval palace, a fairy tale castle, home to a handsome young prince and his blond bride? Is it a cathedral? No. Despite having a statue of Christ surmounting the end wall of what could be a nave, it is not a cathedral, for this 'nave' is aligned north-south. This building is an example of a Victorian definition of beauty: the ornamental concealment of use. Behind the cascade of turrets, towers and Arts-and-Crafts inspired ironwork are the Royal Courts of Justice ('the Law Courts').

Above the west side of the main entrance is a statue of Moses, the law-giver, and above the east, a statue of Alfred the Great. The only English king to be called 'Great', Alfred has been regarded as 'the Wise King', the 'Truthteller'.

As a young man he led the West Saxons in a successful campaign against the Danes and restored London as the capital city, although not without destroying what remained of Roman London (Saxon London prior to the capture of the city was in what is now Covent Garden).

In the Royal Courts of Justice (the High Court in England and Wales), can be found the eminent judges who make judicial interpretations of civil law and sit in the Court of Appeal. The arguments offered and the procedures enacted in this building are the culmination of years of struggle to establish concepts of justice.

Anglo-Saxon society was made up from classes of freemen and slaves; indeed slaves were still being bought, sold and traded in English ports until the twelfth century. Some freemen were bound to work on the land of others (Alfred fixed the holidays they were to be allowed). Therefore, an individual's freedom was checked by a dependence on an overlord: individual freedom as a modern idea did not take root until the seventeenth century. The family, or kindred, was the unit of Anglo-Saxon society; not a creation of the state but an element existing prior to the state's creation.

Anglo-Saxon courts were held in the open. Here family conflicts would have been aired, and later, as the state evolved, the conflict between family customs and state laws. The principal means of proof was the oath, not to the truth of fact, but to the claim of defence as a whole, a case of 'making one's law'. The burden of proof was on the accuser, who had no counsel – that was available to the defendant – and should the accuser fail to convince the judge, he would be fined or imprisoned. Penalties usually took the form of financial compensation, *wergild*, the amount to be paid being based on status and therefore ability to pay. This court, the *folc-gemot*, was supplemented by county courts and hundred (a division of a county) courts. For the more local affairs of tenants, courts were held in the house of a lord, the *halimote*, which would acquire greater importance under the Normans.

When, in 1066, the crop-headed, chain-mailed, expert cavalrymen led by William the Conqueror invaded they brought with them French and feudal law. *Feodum* was the inherited right of absolute ownership or tenure; a complex of rights of ownership, use and disposal of property. The Normans destroyed the Saxon culture and imposed a feudal yoke on freeborn Saxons, but Norman law was never able to displace the earlier traditions entirely. Under their rule money payments gave way to punishment in prison. And as they had no written law, law was evoked by concrete cases rather than abstract doctrine. A uniquely Norman procedural introduction was the ordeal of battle; the case could be proved by the outcome of a trial of strength and martial skill. They also introduced the sworn inquest, an early form of jury trial.

Perhaps the most enduring legacy of Norman law is in the language of law, which is riddled with French terms such as estate, tenement, manor, mortgage, lease, tort, slander, heir, marriage, burglary, plaintiff, suit, pleadings, oath, etc. The King's Court, the Curia Regis, is also of Norman origin. This was the only court the King sat in, and it dealt only with great causes and great men. The pleas of lesser men were heard in the Shire Courts by Sheriffs (from Shire Reeve, a county justice). By the time of Henry II the King's Council was the court which tried all crimes and some civil actions in the course of royal progresses around the country. This formed the basis of common law and the Common Law Courts: common law is judge-made law based on earlier local traditions and the practices of the Anglo-Saxon courts.

Unsurprisingly the first court to emerge with a separate identity was the Court of Exchequer, which decided on matters brought to the court by writs served by the King's secretary, the Lord Chancellor, and arising from the payment of taxes to the King. This was followed by the Court of Common Pleas, where matters arising between subjects would be dealt with. Magna Charta (1215) had allowed this court to be held in a fixed place rather than follow the King's Court. The place chosen was Westminster. The Great Charter of Henry III, in 1234, restated this position.

Edward I was appointing attorneys and apprentices of law and although the location of the Court of Common Pleas was fixed, the King's Bench and Exchequer courts still followed the King. An Order in Council of Edward in 1292, 'De Attornitas et Apprenticiis', made to secure the recruitment of an adequate number of apprentices, is the basis of today's judiciary. While the Inns of Court came into being after Common Pleas had been severed from the other courts, the right of judges to prescribe who should practise in the courts – a right they exercise even today – is much older than the first appearance of advocates: only barristers can plead in court.

A system based on six circuits displaced the royal progresses, with Assizes held twice yearly and Quarter Sessions. The King's Bench could however compel a defendant to appear at Westminster when the other courts were not sitting. This enabled him to be tried in the more awesome surroundings of the seat of royal power, but at great personal expense, as he would have to remain in the vicinity of the court for as long as necessary.

The Supreme Court of Judicature now comprises the Court of Appeal, the High Court and the Crown Court; the Royal Courts in the Strand house the first two and are concerned with civil jurisdiction. The 1875 Judicature Act combined the earlier courts into a High Court comprising courts of Chancery, Probate & Divorce, Admiralty, Common Pleas, Exchequer and Queen's Bench. Two years before the present building was opened in 1882, Common Pleas and Exchequer were absorbed by the Queen's Bench.

By 1866 the courts in Westminster had become over-crowded and a competition was held for a new design to be built on the Strand. Eleven architects submitted proposals and with reluctance George Street's design was accepted in 1868. The slums where it was to be located were demolished and building began. Street died in 1881 and the work was completed by his son.

In the main hall of the High Courts (NB no cameras are allowed inside the building) is a statue of Street who was a member of the Oxford Ecclesiological Society and an expert in English thirteenth-century Gothic architecture. He had built a number of churches in his career, but never a cathedral. One glance at the hall is proof enough that he achieved his life's ambition, for this is nothing but a cathedral nave. It was considered to be a waste of space and inappropriate to a court, but this might be as close to heaven as most lawyers will get. A frieze at the base of Street's statue depicts his craftsmen at work, mostly dressed in medieval costume, and contains the only statue of Justice to be found in the court.

Also in the hall is a statue of Sir William Blackstone, which was a gift from the American Bar Association in 1924. Blackstone (1723–80) went to Oxford University at the age of fifteen, obtained a degree and entered Middle Temple in 1741. Called to the bar in 1746 he was not a success, 'not being happy in a graceful delivery or a flow of elocution, nor having any powerful friends or connections to recommend him.' His fame is as the foremost exponent of eighteenth-century law. His *Commentaries*, a survey of English law, first published in 1765 and still read today, were based on lectures and studies. Almost as many copies were sold in America as in England and led Jefferson to want him 'uncanonized', as 'a student finds there a smattering of everything and his indolence easily persuades him that if he understands that book he is master of the whole body of the law.'

Blackstone knew that the drama in the court room should be dominated by the spectacle of the judge, 'the novelty and very parade of . . . [their] appearance have no small influence upon the multitude.' The scarlet robes trimmed with ermine and full-bottomed wigs, which evoked scorn from William Hogarth, were designed to induce awe in the common man. The exhibition of legal costume in the Royal Courts is testimony to the endurance of Blackstone's belief. On display are the robes of a Lord Chief Justice, resplendent and majestic.

The Master of the Rolls, whose robes are also on exhibition, is the senior judge in the Court of Appeal, which has fourteen Lords Justice. The ultimate appeal court in England and Wales is the House of Lords, with its judicial committee known as the Privy Council.

Lastly, there are the clothes of a barrister, the wig, black gown and tie. A judge can refuse an audience with a barrister if he or she is not properly dressed. Senior barristers are known as QCs, Queen's Counsels, or 'silks' on account of the silk gown they wear. Each year a few hundred barristers apply to become QCs: about sixty will be appointed by Letters Patent from the Lord Chancellor. They are selected after examination of records kept by the Lord Chancellor's office. Judges are selected from QCs by a secret procedure known only to the judges.

Due to the increasing sophistication of law and commerce in the eighteenth century, an act was passed in 1728 to allow a new type of lawyer, one whose concern was not advocacy in court, but the preparation of contracts and leases – solicitors. In 1739 they formed 'The Honourable Society of Practitioners in the Courts of Law and Equity'. There is now a clear demarcation between the two types of lawyer. Solicitors are more numerous, about fifty thousand, and there is a higher percentage of women solicitors than barristers.

The solicitor is responsible for preparing a case, and may appear in magistrate's and county courts, but only a barrister can plead when a judge is sitting. The barrister is not the agent of a defendant, cannot be sued for incompetence, and cannot talk to the defendant unless a solicitor is present. Neither, unlike solicitors, can barristers form partnerships: they are self-employed individuals. A QC, in most courts, must lead, that is be assisted by another barrister.

This archaic but cosy arrangement has not surprisingly been criticized, not least on grounds of expense. The present Lord Chancellor, Lord Mackay, issued three green papers for discussion and a Bill is currently being debated in Parliament. It proposes to allow some solicitors to obtain licences in advocacy, for barristers to be allowed to charge contingency fees, and that conveyancing be open to non-lawyers. Lord Mackay has never been a member of the English Bar; he is Scottish and was trained in the Scottish system which is quite separate from English law. Historically, the Lord Chancellor was the King's secretary, today he is appointed by the government of the day and is the head of the legal system. He is responsible for all judicial appointments in England and

Wales, from lay magistrates to High Court judges. The Prime Minister, with advice from the Lord Chancellor, is responsible for appointments to the Court of Appeal and the House of Lords. 'The law is the embodiment of everything that is excellent, it has no kind of fault or flaw, and I my Lords, embody the Law', wrote W.S. Gilbert of the Lord Chancellor in *Iolanthe*.

The proposed changes have been met with squeals of protest; a hundred High Court judges found no disagreement in principle, but stated they would not admit to court an advocate who was not self-employed or had prepared the case, in other words, no solicitor advocates. Barristers argue that advocacy is a special skill and that from the eighteenth century courts were places for learned counsel to display their eloquence and erudition. It was, and still is, argued that for the law to be effective it must be determinate. Thus the punctilious attention to forms, legalistic exchanges between counsel and judge, whose purpose is not to determine the truth of a case, but to establish whether the prosecution has proved, in law, the defendant's guilt beyond reasonable doubt, with the evidence presented in court. Law becomes something more than the sum of its visible parts.

The special skill of an advocate is more than his questioning and argument: there is also an audience in court, the jury and public. Charles Wilkins was a notorious Victorian barrister, renowned for his lack of knowledge of the law. His excuse for drinking stout at midday was that he wanted to fuddle his own brain down to the intellectual standard of an English jury. When defending a man accused of poisoning his wife, Wilkins declared, 'Imagine the thoughts in this man's mind. Her body has been mangled in order to furnish tests of my guilt. That body which I almost worshipped has been torn to pieces and submitted to inspection to meet the requirements of justice!' The defendant fainted and was acquitted by the jury.

If all this talk of the law has fuddled the reader's brain then some fresh air can be taken in Lincoln's Inn Fields. Here can be found an early example of the development of the West

End. Before the area was developed it was two 'waste common fields', Purse Field and Cup Field, lying north of Fickett's Field. Evidence of its rural nature can be found in the two quaint timber-framed farm labourers' cottages in Portsmouth Street. There is a myth that timber-framed buildings used old ship's timbers, but there is no evidence for this. The cottages date from 1567 and are reputed to be those immortalized by Charles Dickens in *The Old Curiosity Shop*. The original Old Curiosity Shop was demolished, but Dickens knew this shop well; it was where his bookbinder lived with his daughter, the probable inspiration for Little Nell. Today it is an antique shop with a small Dickens museum.

Purse Field was acquired by Sir Charles Cornwallis in 1613 and he sought permission to build on it. However, the lawyers of Lincoln's Inn objected and argued that for their 'general Commoditie and health' the field should 'be converted into walkes'. The idea was commended by Charles I, but he lost his head before the developers could be frustrated. In the 1630s William Newton acquired both fields and agreed that 'for ever and hereafter' the main part of the fields 'be open and unbuilt'. On the west side of the square a house, No 59–60, built by Newton survives. Dating from *circa* 1640 it has been attributed to Inigo Jones. The house next to it, No 57–58, was built nearly a century later by an admirer of Jones's Palladian style, and was where John Forster, Dickens's biographer and friend lived. Nos 12, 13 and 14, on the north side were owned by Sir John Soane, the architect of the Bank of England. His greatest distinction as an architect of London is that more of his buildings have been demolished than anyone else's. He built No 12 in 1792, No 13 in 1812 and No 14 in 1824, residing at No 12 from 1792 to 1812. But this was never intended to be just a house, he was also building a museum. The façade of this museum, a striking feature (which was open until glazed by Soane in 1834), shows his kleptomania: the Gothic pedestals built into the piers between the windows come from the fourteenth-century north front of Westminster Hall. The museum houses a remarkable collection of Egyptian, Roman, Greek, Medieval, Renaissance and Oriental objects, a fascinating 'Aladdin's Cave'. William Hogarth's *Rake's Progress* and *The Election* are on show in the picture room.

Hogarth, engraver, draughtsman, painter and satirist, was an influential artist of his age. Under the patronage of Thornhill (painter of the ceiling of St Paul's), whose daughter he married, he changed from silver engraver to a critic of the dehumanizing money values, cultural snobbery and Palladianism of his time; creating paintings of the crowd which used real people, people who get in each other's way, people whose breath smells. In his own words he says, 'I therefore turned my thoughts to a still more novel mode, viz. painting and engraving modern moral subjects. . . . I wished to compose pictures on canvas, similar to representations on the stage. . . . I have endeavoured to treat my subjects as a dramatic writer; my picture is my stage, and men and women are my players. . . . This I found was most likely to answer my purpose, provided I could strike the right passions, and by small sums for many, by the sale of prints I could engrave from my own pictures, thus secure the property to myself.'

He painted *The Rake's Progress* in 1732–33. The engravings followed in 1735. Mrs Soane paid £570 for the paintings at Christie's in 1802. These paintings have to be 'read' and made novelists like Fielding use their eyes.

The first is titled *The Heir*. Master Tom Rakewell has just inherited his father's fortune. The name is a pun, the father was a niggardly miser, he raked money well. Tom, in melodramatic tradition, will become a spendthrift and rake, the antithesis of his father. Behind Tom sits a lawyer, who no doubt helped to make the miser rich, already stealing from the open purse. A housemaid has discovered a cache of money in the chimney breast. Standing with her mother is the distressed Sarah Young. Rakewell has made her pregnant, but not wishing to marry her is offering them money. However, the focal point of the scene is the tape measure held by the tailor against Tom's leg. This is not a simple moral tale of debauchery, Hogarth is more subtle than that: Tom's decline is due to his slavish following of fashion.

In the next scene, *The Levee*, Tom is attending a morning meeting where scholars discuss art, in particular the art of the old European masters. A Handelian musician is playing the piano. There are fencing-masters and dancing-masters. All are here to teach the young man of fashion what he needs to make his way. Because they dressed in Italian-inspired clothes they were popularly known as 'Macaronis'. It is these self-appointed arbiters of good taste who will lead Rakewell to destruction. To attack this cultural snobbery Hogarth made and sold engravings of most of his work.

In *The Orgy* Tom, after a night of brawling with the watch, is looking to satisfy his sexual desires. The scene is set in the Rose Tavern, Covent Garden, which, like many eighteenth-century pubs, ran a 'cock and hen club' (a brothel) as a lucrative sideline. Hogarth is not condemning Tom for his desires, the picture is quite sensual, but the blank expression on his face may be due to more than drunkenness. Although he may already have contracted syphilis (a pot of pills is spilt on the floor), his blank face is due to his not enjoying what he's doing. He is at the brothel because that is what a young man should do. The young lady is a posture dancer, she uses a polished salver, a candle, and wears no clothes for her act. The walls of the room are hung with portraits of Roman emperors, of which only Nero's has not been defaced.

A man of fashion has not made his way until he has been presented at St James's Palace. But before Tom arrives, his past overtakes him: he is arrested for debt. The ever loyal Sarah, who has been working as a humble seamstress and saving all she can, is able to pay off his creditors. While his release in *The Arrest* is being negotiated, the careless, or mischievous, lamplighter spills oil on Tom's fine clothes.

Seeking ways to restore his fortune, Tom happens upon an advertisement in a newspaper. A rich widow wishes to find a new husband. In *The Marriage*, set in St Marylebone Church, Tom stands in front of the altar with his wife-to-be, a one-eyed crone. Sarah can be seen standing at the back of the church carrying their baby in her arms. Tom could do the honourable thing, leave now and marry Sarah, but he needs money. The clergyman is only too willing to oblige. He stands in front of an inscription of the Ten Commandments which has a crack running through it, and there are cobwebs over the poor box.

Many pubs were also houses of call, places to find employment and places to be paid off in. Wages were often kept back until late on Saturday night and then would soon be spent behind the bar or gambled away at the tables. This was an arrangement which suited employers and publicans alike. But *The Gaming House* was a little more upmarket. As Tom kneels in despair, a fortune squandered again, a nobleman is securing an advance from a money-lender. He is surrounded by men obsessed by gambling, most of whom have failed to notice that the room is about to burn down.

The Prison is now the inevitable setting. Tom, arrested for debt, is in the Fleet Prison. A prison chamberlain ran the prison to make a profit; all accommodation, food and drink would have to be paid for. Tom has tried selling a play to John Rich, the owner of Lincoln's Inn Field Theatre: the returned manuscript lies on a table. Sarah has fainted, having realized that Tom is losing his mind. In the back of the cell is a four-poster bed with wings attached: Tom is having flights of fancy. There are books on alchemy around the cell walls and a telescope pointing through the bars of a window at the heavens.

Tom's life comes to its end, with him lying naked on the floor of *The Madhouse*. Surrounded by inmates representing the follies of the world — a madman posing as a saint, a mad monk, a urinating man wearing a crown — he is furtively admired by a well dressed lady and her less coy maid. The well dressed woman is passing the afternoon being amused, for a few pence, in the madhouse. Tom is released from his chains. Sarah weeps over a man who, seduced by the men of fashion, ends his life a mad bankrupt.

Hogarth also satirized the political scene. His 'Election' series, bought by Soane in 1823 for 1,650 guineas, does not reveal the artist's political affiliation but his contempt for all politicians. Painted in 1754, the four paintings depict a particularly corrupt election which took place in Oxfordshire that year, the first in the county for forty years. They portray the muddled nature of the idea of the freeborn Englishman. On the one hand he is a townsman, a member of the crowd, free from the servitude of the agricultural worker. On the other he is himself a robust countryman contemptuous of the fops and conniving politicians in London.

The contest between the Tory (or Country Party as many squire MPs preferred to call it) and a local Whig magnate results in a narrow victory for the Tory. Every scene has references to the absurdity of political slogans and the immorality of politics. The candidate, while supporting the anti-semitic Jew Bill, buys trinkets from a Jewish trader, a blind man is shown going to the poll, Britannia's coach, led by cheating card-playing coachmen, is about to crash in the river. The Tory comes face to face with his own future, a skull, as he is lifted up in a victory procession.

In real life he was unseated by the Whig-dominated House of Commons on charges of intimidation and corruption.

To the east of Lincoln's Inn Fields, and having the appearance of an Oxbridge college, is Lincoln's Inn. The somewhat unimaginatively named New Square, a speculative development and orginally not a part of the Inn, dates from the late seventeenth century. Old Buildings, (formerly known as Gatehouse Court), of attractive red brick, and home of the Honourable Society, were erected between 1490 and 1520. The history of the Honourable Society is very well documented from 1422 in the Black Books (records of the Inn) and these indicate that students must have been admitted before 1420. From 1422 the society was paying rent to the Hospital of Burton Lazars, and also to the Bishops of Chichester until 1553. Bishop Sherbourne demised 'all that great house' to William Sulyard, for ninety-nine years, in 1535. But the following year his successor, Bishop Sampson, conveyed the house to William and Edward Sulyard. Edward then conveyed the premises to Richard Kingsmill 'and all the rest of the Masters of the Bench of the House and their heirs' in 1580. Rent was paid to the Sulyard family between 1536 and 1580, and the title of the Inn was confirmed by Charles I in 1635.

But if the tenure is well documented the origins of the society and the derivation of its name, are more uncertain. It is most likely named after Henry de Lacy, the third Earl of Lincoln. The earl was a close friend and adviser to Edward I and had some influence on the Order in Council of 1292 for the training of law apprentices. He was appointed in 1298 to arrange the marriage between Edward, Prince of Wales and Isabella of France. However, the Earl of Lincoln's Inn was located on the corner of Shoe Lane and was known as Strange's Inn by 1417; the earl's daughter, Alesia, having married Ebulo Strange around 1322–25. Part of the present site was the estate of John Herlycun, forfeited to Henry III and granted by him to Ralph Neville, Bishop of Chichester, in 1226–27. Part of the Bishop's Inn was discovered when the west extension of the chapel was built in 1877. Lawyers may have shared part of the Bishop's Inn from about 1340 to 1412–13.

Alumni of the Inn were Oliver Cromwell, William Penn and Jeremy Bentham. Bentham was a jurist and utilitarian philosopher. He argued for a legal code which was precise, consistent and wholly enforced, contrary to the personalized and paternalistic justice of the eighteenth century. Hailed as a prophet of nineteenth-century freedom, he was concerned with the regulation, if not the conditioning, of social behaviour. Good actions should be rewarded by the correctly proportioned amount of pleasure, bad by measured amounts of pain. Prisons, a more suitable laboratory to test his ideas, should humiliate the inmates. With their name and prison indelibly printed on their faces, men and women would be put to hard labour in a building he called a 'panopticon', designed so an overseer could see all that went on in the circular building. His ideas influenced Lord Brougham, also a member of Lincoln's Inn, who as Lord Chancellor introduced reforms in the legal system, and the Reform Act of 1832.

William Penn's contribution to English justice came

indirectly through his arrest on charges of causing an affray. The jury at the Old Bailey trial was directed by the judge to find Penn guilty. Instead they acquitted him, were fined and imprisoned by the judge to force a change of verdict. One of the jurors appealed against the judge's action, and what is known after him as the Bushell Case (1670) established, by a ruling of Lord Chief Justice Vaughan, the independence of juries.

Charles Dickens refers to the Old Hall of Lincoln's Inn in *Bleak House*. He describes a fog swirling around Temple Bar:

> ... at the very heart of the fog, sits the Lord High Chancellor in his High Court of Chancery.
> Never can there come fog too thick, never can there come mud and mire too deep, to assort with the groping and floundering conditions which this High Court of Chancery, most pestilent of hoary sinners, holds, this day, in the sight of heaven and earth.

Inside, the case of *Jarndyce* v. *Jarndyce* 'drones on' for forty years, only coming to an end when one side of the family runs out of money and can no longer pay the lawyers. But of course, 'a poor man has nothing more to fear from lawyers than from a gang of pickpockets'.

In 1827, at the age of sixteen, Dickens joined the law firm of Ellis and Blackmore in Gray's Inn, 1 South Square. Here he first acquired a contempt for the law and lawyers that he was to hold for the rest of his life.

Thomas Bowles's 1744 map of London shows Gray's Inn just north of Lincoln's Inn, at the northern limit of the built-up area, open to the north but enclosed by development on the remaining sides. Gray's Inn was the most rural of the Inns of Court and felt the effect of the most outstanding of the late seventeenth century speculative property developers, Nicholas Barbon. Gifted with charm that barely concealed arrogance, and a persuasiveness sugared with blandishments and financial inducements that was deceitful and ultimately brutal, he introduced standardization and mass production into the service of the developer. His clear understanding of the relationship between use and value, value and price, and the significance of currency, credit and interest was quoted by Marx in *Capital*.

On his return from Leyden, where he had studied medicine, he rebuilt the burnt-out house of his father in Crane Court, Fleet Street. Behind its distinctive new façade, in an elegantly furnished drawing-room, he met with owners and tenants of properties he wished to redevelop. First he would win over the most vocal and then propose his terms. Those foolish enough to resist would find their houses pulled down around their ears.

In 1674 he purchased and developed Essex House, south of the Strand. He tore down the great Tudor mansion and dug up the gardens which were terraced down to the river. Charles I was meanwhile attempting to repurchase the property, at a higher price than Barbon had paid, to make a gift of it to Arthur Capel, recently made Earl of Essex. The king failed. Devereux Court, off Essex Street, and New Court in the Middle Temple are examples of Barbon's work. Barbon, according to the lawyer Roger North, knew how to handle lawyers, giving them buildings 'to serve not only our occasions but our fancies'. He built several blocks of chambers in the Temple.

The lawyers of Gray's Inn had long appreciated their rural setting with its views of the hills to the north and the open space to the west known as Red Lyon Fields. Mindful of the loss of Lincoln's Inn Fields, they were dismayed by Barbon's newest and most ambitious scheme. In 1684, around a laid out piazza in Red Lion Square, he began to build terraced houses for the gentry. In protest, one hundred members of Gray's Inn, putting aside their robes, rolled up their sleeves and engaged in a pitched battle with Barbon's workmen. Bricks from the newly laid foundations were hurled, punches thrown and the lawyers made off with two labourers as hostages. The next day Barbon marched his men around the field and warned that he could call on a thousand or more men; the building went ahead.

Despite making a fortune initiating fire insurance and

property developments he owed enormous debts when he died in 1698. Typically, his will instructed that none of his debts should be paid.

Boisterousness was perhaps not unusual in the members of Gray's Inn. Elizabeth I felt compelled, in 1574, to direct 'that every man of the Society should trane and reform himself for the manner of his apparel according to the proclamation then last set forth, and within the time therein limited, else not be accounted of this house; and·that none of this society should wear any gown, doublet, hose or other outward garments, of any light colour, upon penalty of expulsion.' Other rules stipulated that no hats, boots or spurs were to be worn at meals; that no laundresses or women called victuallers under forty years of age were to be allowed in the Inn; that there should be no standing with the back to the fire.

Lady Bacon, writing to her son Francis in 1594, wrote 'I trust they will not mum nor masque nor sinfully revel at Gray's Inn.' While he held some of his mother's puritan views, he was to revel at Gray's Inn, most famous of all the Inns for its Saturnalian festivities. The first recorded revel took place in 1525, compiled by John Roo: it was widely praised by all except Cardinal Wolsey whom it caricatured. But that was the purpose of the revel, a theatrical display of unrestrained licence in which lords and masters acted as humble servants, and servants ruled in an often riotous student prank. Gray's Inn records were destroyed by fire on 22 January 1687 during the revels.

James I was guest of honour in 1613 at a revel presented by Bacon. The members appeared as Iris, the personification of the rainbow, Mercury, the conductor of the dead to Hades, sea-green nymphs, sky-coloured Hyades and flame-coloured Cupids. Then Flora, the goddess of flowers introduced the rustic dance of Pedant, whose pretentious learning and strict adherence to formal rules of scholarship are mocked by the May-Lord, youth and gaiety, together with the Serving-Man, Chambermaid, Country Clown and Country Wench, Host and Hostess, a He-Baboon and a She-Baboon, the He-Fool and the She-Fool. This was intended as a comic interlude to be followed by the more serious entertainment, which today would probably also raise a laugh: twelve Olympic Knights in carnation satin embroidered with silver stars emerged from two golden pavilions and closed the revel with dancing and a farewell song. An equally surreal and comic sight occured in 1733 when the Master of the Revels took the Lord Chancellor, resplendent in ceremonial costume, by the right hand, and with the left, Justice Pope, red robed with a full-bottomed wig, and, holding hands together with all the other serjeants, danced around the open fire in the middle of the hall.

The humour could also be verbal. In 1566, *The Supposes* (Gascoine) was presented: 'I suppose you are assembled here', the prologue says, 'supposing to reap the fruit of my travails and, to be plain, I mean presently to present you with a comedy called *Supposes*, the very name whereof may peradventure drive into every of your heads a sundry suppose to suppose the meaning of our supposes. . . . But understand this our suppose is nothing else but the mistaking or imagination of one thing for another, for you shall see the master supposed for the servant, the servant for the master. . . .'

The presentation in 1594 was called *The History of the High and Mighty Prince Henry, Prince of Parpoole.* The Inn was part of the manor of Portpool, first mentioned in 1308, the residence of Sir Reginald le Grey, Chief Justice of Chester. It became an Inn sometime in the fourteenth century.

The hall, scene of the revels and readings, was built in 1556. It and Middle Temple Hall are the only two buildings extant in which Shakespeare's plays were performed in his lifetime. *The Comedy of Errors* was first staged in Gray's Inn Hall in 1594. Both Gray's Inn Hall and Middle Temple Hall were damaged by bombs in the Second World War. There are other links between the two Inns. Apart from the purely topographic (Gray's Inn is linked to Inner Temple by Chancery Lane), the Griffin of Gray's Inn can be found on Inner Temple garden gate, and the Pegasus of Inner Temple is over Gray's Inn gateway. Both Inns had spectacular revels which were occasionally joint productions.

Francis Bacon's thought influenced ideas during the 1640s. He believed that by experiment, manual labour and co-operative effort, Eden might be recreated on earth, and that mankind could create a better life. He hoped to realize his sound vision by breaking down the barriers between laymen and professionals; by teaching in English and not Latin; and by placing an emphasis on *things* and the practical rather than words and theories. He was said by Henry Stubbe to have so inspired Englishmen with 'such a desire of novelty as rose to a contempt' of church and state that he was responsible for the civil war. Perhaps because he felt that nature cannot 'be commanded except by being obeyed' he supervised the planting of Gray's Inn garden in 1597, planting a catalpa tree, the seed of which was brought from America by Ralegh.

Clearly Dickens was not impressed by the revels or the gardens: 'Indeed, I look upon Gray's Inn generally as one of the most depressing institutions in brick and mortar known to the children of men.' (*The Uncommercial Traveller*). In 1834 Dickens was living in Furnival's Inn, a little way to the east. The site is now occupied by a coral pink brick building of 1879, Waterhouse's design for the Prudential Insurance company.

The thoroughfare that connects the four Inns of Court is Chancery Lane, formerly Chancellor's Lane. At the northern end is the 'Drill Hall' of the Lawyer's regiment, five hundred of whom marched to the defence of Charles I. The official motto of the regiment is 'Retained for the Defence', but George III preferred to call them 'The Devil's Own'.

The lawyer's outfitters, Ede and Ravenscroft, suppliers of wigs, robes, patent leather buckled shoes and black silk stockings, have premises on the Lane. The Law Society, the professional association of solicitors, is housed in an 1831 building opposite the Public Records Office Museum. The site occupied by the museum covers Serjeant's Inn, dissolved in 1876, and the former house of the Keeper of the Rolls of Chancery. It was demolished in 1896 to make way for the present building, intended as a repository for records of government and the courts of law dating back to the Norman Conquest. The mock Tudor building now only contains medieval records, State Papers prior to 1782 and legal records. The museum contains Shakespeare's will and the Domesday Book. The latter is a survey 'to ascertain how many hundreds of hides of land there were in each shire, and how much land and livestock the king himself owned . . . and what annual dues were lawfully his from each shire. . . .' (*Anglo-Saxon Chronicle*). There are two volumes in the Public Records Office Museum. The Great Domesday is written in a single English hand of the last of the clerics who had organized the Saxon court. It reveals that twenty years after the Conquest there were few Englishmen with influence over the King, and that, while life for the peasants and free farmers was changed very little (they simply paid rent to new masters), the Saxon thegns had had their land taken from them to reward five thousand or more Norman and French nobles and soldiers of fortune by a king who never learned English. Feudalism had arrived.

The half-timbered building of 1610–11 above Inner Temple Gateway is known as Prince Henry's Room, after the elder son of James I, and was probably the Council Chamber of the Duchy of Cornwall.

The upheavals of the seventeenth century inflicted fatal wounds in the feudal body; commerce was becoming the basis of land ownership, and a nobility of merchants displaced the feudal lords. But it was a protracted death. The reinstated Stuart kings, Charles II and James II, attempted to wrest power back from Parliament and revive the divine right of kings. The struggle between Anglicans, Catholics and Dissenters continued and a new form of monarchy evolved – the constitutional monarch.

Many of the public manifestations of these changes occurred around the Temple Bar. The pro-Stuart Jacobite, Francis Towneley, had his head exhibited over the gateway in 1746. Defoe, because of his satirical writing, was locked up in the prison above; he was given food and flowers by an admiring mob. The printers' workshops on Fleet Street were the source of many political and satirical pamphlets, attacking corrupt politicians, Whig or Tory, 'For 'tis such rogues as these corrupted the nation/ And caused the disturbances, strife and vexation.' Around Temple Bar the cry 'Wilkes and Freedom' went up from the mob that only found freedom in the street:

> No ignorant coxcombs but good politicians
> Such as Wilkes, H, G, S, and T, D
> True to country and king and in freedom abounding
> Huzza my brave boys may the king live forever
> To old England's glory this would be more clever
> The above mentioned gentry so long birds of a feather
> To hell without heads, go all dancing together.

John Wilkes was a radical politician who was arrested for an alleged libel on the King, and who, despite being elected three times, was not allowed to take his seat in Parliament. He was a friend of Hogarth, whose interpretation of the essential paradox of eighteenth century society led to a bitter quarrel between them. Wilkes accused Hogarth who had been steadily moving toward the court and an enlightened monarchy, of giving up 'the rare talents of gibbeting in colours'.

There are no crowds shouting for liberty around Temple Bar today, just office workers and lawyers and visitors. But there are also traditions; every November the Lord Mayor of London, in a ceremony with roots in the Anglo Saxon Folkmoot, passes Temple Bar on his way to the Law Courts to be sworn in before the Queen's Justices; and whenever the Queen, in her official capacity, visits the City she will find Temple Bar closed. She is met by the Lord Mayor who presents her with the City's Pearl Sword, this in recognition of her sovereignty outside the City. She touches the handle, accepting the Mayor's authority within the City and under his protection she enters Temple Bar. All the history surrounding Temple Bar has been distilled to a genteel stroke from a royal finger.

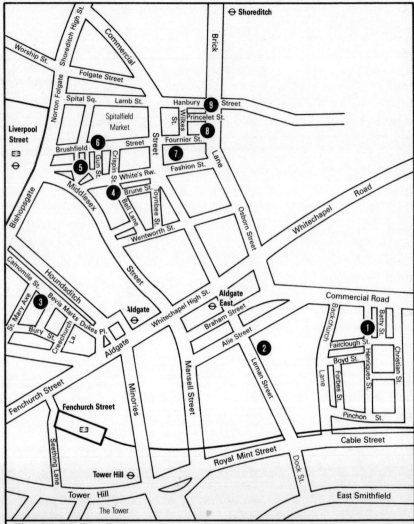

The Jewish East End

1 Henriques Street (formerly Berners Street). Rudolf Rocker founded the International Workers' Education Club, commonly known as the Anarchists' Club, in this street.

2 Leman Street. Now long gone, The Poor Jews' Temporary Shelter was located here; one of several responses to the poverty of Jewish immigrants who had settled in the East End.

3 Bevis Marks. The oldest surviving synagogue in Britain is located here.

4 Brune Street. The Soup Kitchen for the Jewish Poor, located in this street, fed around 5,000 people a week in the 1930s; it still functions.

5 Sandys Row. A synagogue was founded here by Dutch Jews.

6 Gun Street. At no. 40 Aaron Lieberman founded the Hebrew Socialist Union.

7 Fashion Street. Once home to many writers including Wolf Mankowitz and Jack London.

8 Fournier Street/Brick Lane. What began life in 1743 as a Huguenot Chapel, became a synagogue in 1892. Possibly no other building better reflects the changing communities in the area.

9 Princelet Street. Site of the third oldest synagogue in England, currently undergoing careful restoration.

The Soup Kitchen for the Jewish Poor, Brune Street.

The Great Synagogue, Fournier Street, Spitalfields.

A German Bomber, photographed from above, flying during a daylight raid over Tower Hamlets.

Winston Churchill inspecting the bomb damage in the East End.

THE JEWISH EAST END
Roger Tyrrell

London is a vast and ever changing city with nearly two thousand years of history. To the casual visitor there are simply endless streets punctuated by the occasionally interesting building or vista. Yet much is hidden beneath the surface: what does one make for example of street names like Milk Street, Bread Street, Honey Lane, Ironmonger Lane, etc.? The answer is simple: these streets, now entirely populated by banks, were once the market streets of the medieval City of London. But look closer: in the midst of these streets and alleys is one called Old Jewry. What does this signify? Again the answer is as straightforward as with the market streets: the Old Jewry was the street of the Jews, the centre of the medieval Jewish ghetto of the City of London. Beyond the street name it seems there is nothing here to remind us of the past, yet closer inspection will prove that false.

First though, move further east to the very fringe of the City of London, to Aldgate, where once the eastern gate of the city stood. Just inside the old walled area is another street suggestive of the Jewish community, Jewry Street – once known as the Poor Jewry. Not far away in Creechurch Lane a commemorative blue plaque marks the 'Site of the first Synagogue after the Resettlement 1655, Spanish and Portuguese Jews Congregation'. 'Poor Jews', 'Resettlement', these are clues to a rich and fascinating history which the informed eye can read in the streets of London.

Nothing is known of any Jewish communities in England before 1066, though there were probably individual Jewish merchants travelling the country, and possibly some settled groups. The attitude of the Jewish people to England in the medieval period is epitomized by the standard description of England in Jewish literature as the 'end of the earth'! It has long been believed that William the Conqueror invited Jewish merchants from Rouen in Normandy to settle in London, Oxford and York. Whether this was the case or whether they simply followed Duke William under his protection cannot be determined. Fresh impetus to immigration was undoubtedly given by a terrible massacre of Jews at Rouen in 1096 by a passing group of crusading knights.

William I and his son William Rufus appear to have treated the Jews decently, in fact the church accused Rufus of intent to convert to Judaism! However, the position of the merchants was ever precarious: prevented by the Christian guilds from practising any of the trades of the city, barred from owning land, they were only able to practise medicine and moneylending. Both were inherently dangerous occupations in medieval times. For example, in 1130 the entire London community (numbering perhaps two or three hundred) was accused of murdering a sick man. It is most likely that he was treated by a Jewish physician who failed to cure him, but an immense fine of £2,000 was imposed on Rabbi Joseph (known as Rubi Gotsce) for the supposed crime. Documents of the Royal Exchequer show Rabbi Joseph to have been a great financier and a notable scholar. Joseph, along with other businessmen such as Manasser (Menasseh) and Jacob and his wife, had extensive financial dealings with the Abbot of Westminster and the crown.

The very success of the Jewish financiers put them in danger from the church, noblemen, and the kings who were indebted to them. The kings, particularly, were given to reneging on their obligations and also to extorting money from the Jews. In 1144, during the civil war between King

Stephen and the Empress Matilda, both monarchs raised cash from the Jews. Matilda had placed a levy on the Jews of Oxford and, on seizing the city, King Stephen demanded a levy three and a half times that of Matilda. The king forced payment by the simple expedient of burning the Jews' houses one by one until the full sum was paid.

More ominously for the long term future, in 1144 a boy called William was found dead in woods near Norwich. The rumour spread that William had been lured to a synagogue and crucified on the second day of Passover. The sheriff of Norwich gave protection to the Jews in his castle, but one was murdered by a knight who was in his debt. William became venerated as a saint and thus was propagated the idea of ritual murder. This is in fact the first recorded incidence anywhere in Europe of this infamous accusation that would pursue the Jews down the centuries, and so stands as England's own peculiar contribution to the annals of anti-semitism.

The mid-twelfth century begins to yield more names of the Jewish community in London and elsewhere. The London Rolls show Jews from Spain and Morocco, France (Étampes, Joigny and Pontoise), and Jews from Italy (known as 'Lombard') in Winchester. There is even a Jew from Russia. These records show about 300 Jewish businessmen scattered around the country. The leader of the London community until his murder in the coronation massacre of 1189 was Rabbi Jacob of Orleans, a friend and fellow scholar of Rabbi Yomtob of Joigny who was the last to die in the Masada-like mass suicide at Cliffords Tower at York in 1190.

This sad catalogue of atrocities could be continued *ad infinitum* but suffice it to say that by 1270 the condition of the Jews of England had reached such a miserable level that the entire community petitioned the King for permission to leave the country. The King refused. However, by 1290 church pressure condemning usury (despite credit being essential to the operation of the economy) and the King's indebtedness led to the expulsion of the entire community from England. The Jews were allowed to keep any portable valuables, and those who could pay were given safe conduct out of the kingdom. Those who embraced Christianity were deprived of all their goods and sent to the Domus Conversorum (The House of Jewish Converts) which stood in Chancery Lane, where the Public Records Office Museum now stands.

A walk along the street called Old Jewry off Cheapside (first mentioned as the Street of the Jews in 1128) will give clues as to what transpired there. Nowadays a street of banks and the City Police headquarters, all the buildings in the street have square plaques attached to them with the symbols of the various guilds of the City of London: Mercers, Goldsmiths, Grocers, etc. These indicate that these guilds own the land upon which the buildings stand as they have done ever since the great bargain auction of 1290.

The Jews' expulsion was without precedent in European history. Hitherto, expulsions had been local rather than national, and there can be little doubt that it provided both inspiration and a spurious justification for the expulsions from Spain in 1492 and those in Russia in the nineteenth century.

Until 1177 all Jewish burials in England were in the burial ground in London known as the 'Jews' Garden' in Jewin Crescent (now disappeared) in the Barbican area. This burial ground was excavated by Professor Grimes in the 1950s. Grimes found evidence of several hundred burials but no trace of human remains – we can only surmise the bodies were dug up and carried away when the Jews were expelled from England in 1290. The feeling of the Jews towards England was such that they would not even suffer their dead to remain here.

For nearly four centuries after the expulsion it was held that it was illegal for a Jew to reside in England, yet they were here. Successive governments found it expedient to ignore the presence of traders with international experience especially if they were profitable to the crown. During these centuries the Jews in England were either 'conversos' (converts to Christianity) or 'Marranos' (Jews publicly professing Christianity but privately practising Judaism). An early example is Dr Roderigo Lopes, personal physician to Queen

Elizabeth I, executed on patently false charges of treason (there is a list of famous trials displayed in the City of London Guildhall which includes that of Dr Lopes').

The Puritan revolution in England, culminating in the English Civil War of 1642–48, radically altered the position of the Jews *vis-à-vis* England. The revolution, itself an extended process through the reigns of Elizabeth, James I and Charles I, involved a search for purity in religion and, above all, a return to the Bible as a source of authority. Translations of the Bible into English were now available and printing made them widespread. Puritans reading their Bibles were impressed with the religious rigour of the Old Testament prophets and became increasingly interested in Judaism. A chair in Hebrew studies at Oxford was founded to facilitate the more accurate translation of the Bible and soon pamphlets were circulating questioning the exclusion of Jews from England. Suggestions were made that the problems that beset England (as far as the Puritans were concerned, this meant the King and the established church) were God's punishment for the way the Jews had been treated.

The Civil War led to the execution of the King and to England becoming a republic from 1648–1660. The Commonwealth of Oliver Cromwell was interested in developing overseas trade, particularly at the expense of the Dutch Republic and the Spanish crown. The presence in Amsterdam of a wealthy and talented group of international merchants and financiers of Spanish and Portuguese descent was an attractive prize – if they could be persuaded to come to England.... The process was long and at first furtive, beginning about 1650.

The first Marrano (for they were to remain such for a while) to arrive in London appears to have been Diego Rodriguez Arias in 1651, followed in 1653 by Duarte Henrique Alvarez and his nephew Antonio Rodriguez Robles, who lived in Duke's Place at Aldgate, on the eastern edge of the City. In 1654, a future leader of the London Jewish community arrived – David Abrabanel (also known as Manoel Martinez Dormido). Dormido came from Andalusia where he had been a city treasurer and customs and revenue officer. Tortured by the Inquisition, he went to Amsterdam in 1640, becoming a merchant and an intelligencer (i.e. a spy) for Oliver Cromwell. In 1654, Dormido lost his business in Recife due to the exigencies of war and came to live in Great St Helens, London (not far from Aldgate). Dormido formed a minyan in his house and in the year of his arrival petitioned Cromwell for the resettlement of the Jews in England.

The following year (1655) two other future leaders arrived in London – Simon (Jacob) de Caceres and Antonio Ferdinando Carvajal (also known as Abraham Hisquiau Carvajal). Caceres was a merchant and shipowner with interests in the sugar trade and land in Barbados and was a Sephardi, originally from Hamburg. Carvajal was a shipowner and gold bullion merchant born in Portugal at Fundao. He fled to the Canaries in 1630, later joining a Marrano group in Rouen where he was denounced by a certain Diego Cisneros. Carvajal escaped to England in 1655, and settled in Leadenhall Street in the City of London. The same year Carvajal, along with his sons Alonzo, Jorge and Joseph, was endenizened (naturalized) by Oliver Cromwell. Carvajal like Dormido had a minyan at his house but pursued the rather odd disguise of being a Roman Catholic (in a fiercely Protestant country!) by attending mass at the Spanish Embassy. He was fined as a recusant (a persistent Catholic) in 1655. It is difficult to explain Carvajal's behaviour unless it is connected to the fact that he and Caceres, like Dormido, were also intelligence officers for Cromwell.

Now events were to conspire to bring three separate interests to pursue the same objective. In late 1655 England declared war on Spain, and in March the following year the Council of State ordered the seizure of goods of all Spanish subjects. On 14 March two ships belonging to Antonio Robles (Carvajal's nephew) were seized. Robles immediately petitioned the Commissioners of the Admiralty for return of his property on the grounds that he was neither Spanish nor Catholic, but Portuguese and Jewish. For the first time since 1290 there was an acknowledgement in print that a Jew was living in England! On 16 May the Admiralty reported on its investigation and ordered the restitution of Robles' ships. The rest of the Marrano community now acted swiftly and bravely. Led by Carvajal (who had no reason to fear loss of goods since he was naturalized, though supposedly Catholic), they presented on 24 March 1656 a petition to Cromwell entitled 'A Humble Petition of the Hebrews at present residing in this City of London'. The signatories were Rabbi Manasseh ben Israel, David Abrabanel (Dormido), Antonio Carvajal, Abraham Cohen Gonsales, Jacob (Simon) de Caceres, Abraham Israel de Brito (also Domingo Vaez de Brito), and Isaac Lopes Chillon. The petition asked for permission to hold prayers in private houses and for a burial ground outside the city. Cromwell referred the petition to the Council of State who organized a conference at Whitehall. Legal opinion held that the expulsion order of 1290 was an act of royal prerogative affecting only those individuals at that time and that there was no legal impediment to the settlement of Jews in England. However, many counter-arguments were tendered and when it became apparent that no decision would be reached, Cromwell abandoned the conference.

On 24 June 1656, Cromwell summoned the leaders of the Jews to Whitehall and gave them verbal assurances (carefully committing nothing to writing) that they might build a synagogue, acquire a burial ground, trade as brokers on the Royal Exchange and enlarge their community by bringing over 'merchants of good standing' from Amsterdam. It is in this last assurance that Cromwell's motivation is exposed – he was attempting to secure much-needed capital for his republic. Cromwell implicitly recognized the Carvajal, Caceres, Dormido triumvirate as the leaders of the Anglo-Jewish community. The Jews were resettled, but in the bargain they had struck they had broken the heart of their Rabbi Manasseh ben Israel.

Manasseh ben Israel (also Manoel Dias Soeiro), born at Madeira in 1604, was one of the leading Jewish scholars of the seventeenth century. Manasseh lived most of his life in Amsterdam where he became Rabbi of the Great Synagogue.

In 1641 a Marrano named Antonio de Montezinos arrived in Amsterdam with the story that he had travelled to Quito in Ecuador and there encountered members of the lost tribes of Reuben and Levi practising Jewish ceremonies. Montezinos was questioned by an assembly of the Great Synagogue, including ben Israel, and swore an affidavit as to the truth of his allegations. Ben Israel considered the implictions of the 'facts': the Book of Daniel (xii; 7) predicts that Redemption of the Jews will begin only when the scattering of the Jewish people is complete; equally Deuteronomy (xxvii; 64) states that the dispersion was to be universal 'from one end of the earth unto the other'. According to the evidence, the Jews were now to be found in America; the only place they were lacking was England. This idea was reinforced for Manasseh by the fact that England is invariably referred to in medieval Jewish literature as 'the end of the earth' (the result of an over-literal translation of French *Angleterre* – and perhaps a reflection on England's climate!). Manasseh determined to secure the return of the Jews to England.

In 1650, ben Israel expounded his ideas on the Diaspora and Deliverance in his book *Spes Israel* (The Hope of Israel), which was dedicated to the English Parliament. As we have seen, ben Israel was one of the signatories of the petition presented to Cromwell, but he was hoping for a general right of Jews to reside in England, not the comfortable business deal struck by the Marranos. Now at odds with the London Jews he was friendless and destitute, and appealed to Cromwell for help. Cromwell generously responded with a cash grant of £25 and an annual pension of £100 a year. In late 1657 Manasseh returned to Amsterdam to bury his son Samuel Soeiro and himself died a broken man a month later.

Meanwhile Carvajal and Caceres went into action on Cromwell's agreement. In February 1657, Carvajal acquired land in Creechurch Lane (near Aldgate) and built a synagogue for the 'Kahal Kados Sahar Asamaim' – The Congregation Gates of Heaven. Carvajal's cousin, Moseh Israel Athias, became the first Rabbi. In the same month Caceres and Carvajal acquired a 999-year lease on a burial ground,

'Bethahaim Velho', behind No. 253 Mile End Road (east of
the City). In 1663 David Abrabanel Dormido and Eliau de
Lima were elected Parnassim of the congregation with Moseh
Baruh Lousada as Gabay (treasurer). Together they were
instructed to draw up the forty-two Ascamot (laws) of the
synagogue. The Anglo-Jewish community (as it would become known) was established.

At the same time that the wealthy and cultured Sephardim
were emerging from their crypto-Judaism in London, far to
the east events were occurring that would bring an Ashkenazi
community to England. The Chemielnicki Revolt in Poland
between 1648–49 brought in its wake terrible massacres of
Polish Jews who occupied the unfortunate position of
middlemen between the Polish aristocracy and the insurgent
peasants: refugees began to flow westward. Many arrived at
Hamburg, where they became a burden on the charity of the
Ashkenazi and Sephardi congregations, but very early on
adventurous spirits made their way to London.

There are references to Ashkenazim in the Libro de los
Acuerdos (the minute books of the Kahal) of the Creechurch
Lane Synagogue as early as 1667 when Samuel Levy, known
as 'Ribbi Samuel' of Cracow, was appointed beadle (Sha-
mash) of the Great Synagogue, an office he would retain until
1701. In 1675, during reconstruction work at the synagogue,
David Fels and Joseph Tudesco (German) are recorded as
craftsmen. In 1678 Rabbi Raphael ben R. Solomon Zalman
(Lithuanian) is recorded in the Book of Life at the cemetery.
Other references are to Abraham Ashkenazi (1678) and
Joseph Ashkenazi – perhaps the same as Joseph Tudesco?
(1689).

It was in 1669 that the decisive event in the history of the
Ashkenazi community of England occurred with the arrival of
Meir (also Michael) Levy, his brother Moses Levy and Moses'
sons, Benjamin and Seligman (Solomon). Meir who appears
to have been a gifted linguist was appointed 'solicitor' to the
congregation of the Sephardim. Benjamin Levy, the most
illustrious member of the family, was appointed Overseer of
the Poor for the Parish of St Katherine Coleman in 1693, and

in 1697 he became a member of the Royal Exchange (at this time restricted to twelve Jewish members – 'The Jew Brokers'), the only Ashkenazi on the list.

Benjamin and Seligman were endenizened in 1688, and in 1692 Benjamin subscribed to the initial list of shareholders in the Bank of England – the only Jew to do so. In 1693 Benjamin held at least £1,000 in stock of the East India Company. Benjamin was a yahid (full fee paying and voting member of the congregation) at Creechurch Lane and signed the new Ascamot of 1677.

These Ashkenazim worshipped in the Sephardi synagogue, it seems with no compunction. In any case there was no other synagogue available to them. But then, in 1669, Michael Levy was instructed to complain to the Lord Mayor of London of the 'foreign mendicants besetting the synagogue'. In 1678, the congregation resolved that no 'tudesco' could hold office or vote at yehidim meetings, or be called to law, receive honour, pay imposts or make offerings. They made an exception of their beloved shamash Samuel Levy and of Benjamin Levy and his uncle, Meir. Next, in 1682, the congregation ruled that 'foreign tudescos' who came to England to beg charity should be given no more than five shillings and shipped back to Amsterdam.

It was not that the Sephardim were heartless or cruel, they gave a great deal in charity to the Ashkenazim, but they saw no end to the arrival of refugees and no possible means to raise all the money necessary. The records of the following year show large sums being spent on 'repatriating' Ashkenazim in an attempt to circumscribe the limits of charity:

For obtaining the despatch of eight Tudescos and two women £5.12.6.; Given to Izopo (Joseph) the Tudesco to go to Hamburg £0.5.0.

(Accounts of 1679–80)

In 1688 the 'Glorious Revolution' united England and Holland under one king; now there was no obstruction for eager Ashkenazim at Amsterdam wishing to enter Britain. On 14 October 1689 a pass to leave Britain was given to Rabbi

Isaac Cohen Zedek. The timing of the pass, just after important religious festivals, may indicate that Rabbi Isacc had visited England to preach to the Ashkenazim. Whether he did or not, it is certain that within the year the Ashkenazim had founded and built their own synagogue and that the founder, spiritually and financially, was Bejamin Levy.

The records of the Great Ashkenazi Synagogue in Duke's Place, Aldgate, are mainly lost until 1722: all that is left are stray references here and there. Clues arise in the Libro de los Acuerdos: in 1690 Samuel Heilmuth, a jeweller of Duke's Place and hitherto a regular worshipper at Creechurch Lane, ceased attending. In 1692 the Libro refers to the 'Mahamad of the Tudescos' and states that from six months hence no more tudescos other than those paying the finta de Bethahaim would be buried in the house of life. Something had clearly happened and everything points to the foundation of the Great Ashkenazi Synagogue by 1690 at the latest. The Ashkenazim appear to have continued to pay the finta until 1695 when the 'Hebra (Chevra) Kadisha' was founded and Benjamin Levy acquired a 999-year lease on ground abutting the Sephardi cemetery (now part of Alderney Road cemetery, Mile End Road).

Now the two communities (or nations as they refer to themselves in their documents) were established, but initially there were great disparities in their collective wealth. This is illustrated by a levy made for an emissary to the Jews of Lubin, Poland, in 1708; while the Sephardim raised £276.9.0., the Ashkenazim could only collect £5.7.6. But the situation would change over the coming centuries.

In 1701 the Sephardim decided that they needed a new synagogue, a purpose-built one rather than the building they had rented and altered these many years. A site was acquired on Bevis Marks (this is the same street as Duke's Place, it simply changes its name every 100 yards or so), and a Quaker architect and builder, Joseph Avis, was commissioned to design and build the new synagogue. Avis designed the exterior of the synagogue in exactly the manner in which he would have built a Quaker meeting house, and the interior he based on the Great Synagogue at Amsterdam. Having completed the work, Avis charged a very large fee, waited until it was paid, then returned the money saying he did not believe in making money from the works of God. The Bevis Marks synagogue survives to this day, making it the oldest synagogue in England (the Great Synagogue in Duke's Place was destroyed by bombing in World War Two).

The congregation grew, but that of the Sephardim never reached more than several hundred, whereas immigration from the east continually added new members to the Ashkenazi community. By 1700 the Jewish population of England was estimated at 1,000, growing to 8,000 by 1750 and 20–25,000 by 1800. In these years much was achieved. In 1732 the Talmud Torah School was founded by the Great Synagogue, Duke's Place. This would eventually become today's Jewish Free School. In 1760 the two great synagogues founded the Board of Deputies of British Jews in order to represent the congregation to the wider community and forward their rights and interests. In 1708 a dispute arose leading to the first splinter formation within the Great Synagogue, Duke's Place and 'the Hambro' Synagogue was founded. In 1804 a Board of Shechita was founded to ensure that food was prepared in a Kosher manner.

During these years many great families immigrated and joined the congregation of the two synagogues: from Italy in the mid-eighteenth century came the Sephardi Montefiore and Disraeli families, from Germany the Barents Cohens, the Goldsmids and the Rothschilds (Nathan Meyer being the first in 1780). The members of the two synagogues were to become pillars of the English establishment. Many advances were made and by the mid-eighteenth century there was no obstruction to Jewish participation in local government affairs. In 1827 London University was founded to admit Catholics, Nonconformists and Jews alike to higher education: it received much assistance from the Jewish community. In 1833 the first Jew (Sir Francis Goldsmid QC) was called to the bar. In 1835 Sir David Salomons became the first Jewish Sheriff of the City of London and in 1855 Lord Mayor. All that remained now was Parliament.

In 1847 Baron Lionel de Rothschild was elected Member of Parliament for the City of London. The House of Commons had three times passed a bill to allow Jews and Nonconformists to swear the Members' Oath of Allegiance on the book appropriate to their religion, but each time the House of Lords had rejected the bill. Unable to swear the oath, Rothschild sat at the bar of the House of Commons for eleven years (during which time he was re-elected three times by the City) until the Lords finally relented. Lionel swore the oath on the Old Testament Bible and became a full MP. He sat in Parliament for a further fifteen years, never uttering a single word. He said he was happy just to be there.

Further trends towards Anglicization of the two nations during this period were evidenced by the formation of the new synagogue of the Congregation of British Jews of West London. This synagogue, founded in 1842, included members from both 'Great' synagogues who felt alienated from the 'foreign' practices of the older congregations.

Meanwhile, the host community had not ignored the increasing number of Jews in its presence. In the late eighteenth century a collection of fanatically evangelican Christians had founded the London Society for the Promotion of Christianity amongst the Jews. In 1807 the society opened a school for Jewish children and followed this with a larger one at Palestine Place, Bethnal Green, (the site is now occupied by Bethnal Green Hospital) in 1813. Attached to this school was the 'Episcopal Jews Chapel'. The whole complex was opened by the Duke of Kent, father of Queen Victoria. Behind these moves was a general drift in society towards improved education. The Church of England, the Methodist movement and, later, secular organizations were all founding schools to give free education, both religious and secular, to the children of the poor. The London Society was utilizing the desire for eduction, which was as common among Jews as gentiles, to subvert English Jewry.

The Talmud Torah School had already been reorganized in 1788 by Dr Joseph Hart Meyers and was now located in Ebenezer Square, Houndsditch (between Stoney Lane and Gravel Lane). In 1817, it was again reorganized by Dr Joshua van Oven to counter the Christian onslaught and reopened in Bell Lane, Spitalfields, as 'the Jewish Free School'.

Having been defeated in education the London Society now turned to propaganda. In 1813 it founded the journal *Jewish Repository*, which changed its name to *Jewish Expositor and Friend of Israel* in 1816. The problem with these journals was that ill-motivated though they might be, they did contain items of news interest to the Jewish community. The response was the foundation in 1823 of the first Anglo-Jewish newspaper, the *Hebrew Intelligencer*, published by J Wertheimer from 54 Leman Street, Stepney. It does not appear to have lasted long but was followed by others. The big push came in 1841 with two Anglo-Jewish papers appearing simultaneously. One, the *Voice of Jacob* was the result of a proposal of Jacob Franklin, an optician from Portsmouth. Sir Moses Montefiore gave £10 to the enterprise and Baron Lionel de Rothschild £5. The *Voice of Jacob* was published by I Vallentine of Houndsditch and B Steill of Paternoster Row. Its short career may be attributable to the fact that its editors, Dr M J Raphall and David Aaron de Sola (Hazan of Bevis Marks), both spoke English as a foreign language. The same year a better start was made on 12 November 1841, with the first issue of the *Jewish Chronicle* (Sefer Zikkaron). It was published by I Vallentine and edited by Moses Angel (an Ashkenazi and a graduate of London University) and David Meldola (Sephardi, Rabbi, and son of Haham Meldola of Bevis Marks). To this day the *Jewish Chronicle* (popularly known as the *JC*) continues as the principal journal of the English Jewish community.

Fresh impetus to immigration was given by the Bohemian Persecutions of 1744–45, the Haidamack Massacres of 1768, the Decembrist Uprising of 1825 in Russia and the Tsarist crackdown on dissidents that followed, and the pan-European revolutions of 1848 (which brought Karl Marx to England). Yet by 1850 the Jewish population was still only estimated at 35,000. But by 1880 it had nearly doubled to 60,000 and by 1914 it would stand at 250,000.

Initially there was sympathy and concern for the persecuted refugees seeking assistance at the hands of their English co-religionists, but, as with the Sephardim of the seventeenth century, this open-handed attitude was later replaced by the feeling that things could not continue this way indefinitely.

The steady immigration of the first half of the nineteenth century picked up pace in the second half to become a flood after 1881. This year saw the assassination of Tsar Alexander, followed by terrible pogroms in Kiev, Odessa and other cities. Mass immigration of Jews and other minorities persecuted in the Tsarist empire began. This was fuelled over the next few years by increasing penal laws against Jews in Russia and reached a climax with the great pogrom of Kishinev in 1903. The majority of the refugees had their hearts set on the 'goldeneh medina' – the United States – and many reached their goal. But many others made it no further than England, either because they found friends, family or opportunities here, or because they lacked the resources to continue the journey. The 1901 census shows more than 90,000 'Russians and Poles' in the East End. By 1911 there were 106,000 classified in this way, with an additional 20,000 Jews from Romania, Germany, Austria and Holland. It should be remembered that the census does not count children born in this country in the figures. The Aliens Act of 1906 was a panic attempt to stop the influx of refugees, but a fortunate change of government meant it was not seriously applied. The war in 1914 brought the influx to a sudden halt.

Several steps were taken in response to the growing numbers of East European refugees. In 1857 a soup kitchen was founded in Brick Lane, Whitechapel. The soup kitchen was feeding as many as five thousand people a week in the 1930s, and still operates today from its premises in Brune Street, Spitalfields. By January 1858 it was feeding an average of 1,000 people a week. In 1858 the Board of Guardians for the Jewish Poor was founded, drawing on all synagogues for resources.

By the mid-nineteenth century, Anglo-Jewry had moved away from the original area of settlement in Aldgate and was to be found in Marble Arch, Canonbury, Dalston, and other navens of middle class tranquillity. The Aldgate area had become, as had the rest of the City, largely non-residential and filled with warehouses, offices and banks, but the district immediately east of Aldgate was about to become the Jewish area *par excellence*. By 1914, 90 per cent of all Jews in England would live in the crowded streets and alleys of Whitechapel, Spitalfields and St George's in the East. A ghetto was in formation. Why did the refugees choose this area to settle in? One reason was the presence of earlier poor Ashkenazi immigrants in the area, another the existence of the soup kitchen, yet another the existence from 1885 of the Poor Jews' Temporary Shelter in Leman Street. This institution was founded by Hermann Landau (1849–1921). An immigrant, having been born at Constantinov in Poland, he rose to become a Hebrew teacher and, later, a stockbroker. He was awarded the OBE in 1921. Another attraction was the numerous chevrot (societies or clubs based on towns of origin) which existed to aid the newcomer. But above all two factors determined that this distrct would be the ghetto. Firstly, the majority of refugees arrived by steamer from Hamburg and these docked at Irongate Wharf by Tower Bridge (where the Tower Thistle Hotel now stands in St Katharine's Dock); it is a universal wisdom that immigrants first settle where they get off the ship. Secondly, and most decisively, the East End in general was the least desirable part of town, and within the East End the parishes of Spitalfields, Whitechapel and St George's were the least opulent of all. They had no choice, they could not afford alternative accommodation, and would probably not be accepted as tenants elsewhere in any case.

The Jewish communities which had arrived in earlier centuries were, or would become, middle class, but in the nineteenth century working-class Jews were arriving: the earliest identifiable group of Jewish industrial workers were the Dutch Jews who settled in the Cobb Street, Leyden Street and Toynbee Street area of Spitalfields in the 1850s. It was among these workers involved in the cigar and cigarette manufacturing industry that the first strike of Jewish workers in England took place in 1858.

The politics of Anglo-Jewry were changing as immigration proceeded, but at first the change was imperceptible. In 1874 Lewis Smith, a Polish Jewish veteran of the Polish Uprising of 1863 and of the Paris Commune of 1871, came to London. Smith tried to form a union of Lithuanian tailors in Whitechapel. Seventy-two members enrolled, but the union collapsed after a fortnight and Smith went on to New York. This was the first of many attempts to organize the Jewish tailors of East London, but it would be more than thirty years before these attempts were successful.

The East European refugees introduced three elements which had not hitherto been present to any extent in Anglo-Jewry: socialism, trade unionism and Zionism. The Anglo-Jewish community had been very comfortable until the arrival of these strangers who dressed differently, spoke a foreign language (Yiddish) and carried their radical religious or political ideas with them. They were not really welcome, but they were fellow Jews and so, initially, they had to be welcomed. But as early as 1882 the Board of Guardians of the Jewish Poor was taking advertising space in the Jewish press in Russia and Romania warning potential immigrants that if they came to England they would face great hardships and that the Board would give them no relief in the first six months of their residence. The Board was swimming against the tide; the immigrants had no choice but life (if they left) or death (if they stayed), so the hardships of England were as nothing compared to the hardships of home.

The first serious disruption to the politics of Anglo-Jewry was the arrival of Aaron Lieberman in 1875. Lieberman had been expelled from the Rabbinical seminary at Vilna in 1872, on the not unreasonable grounds that he was both an atheist and an anarchist. He was then expelled from the Technological School at St Petersburg in 1875 and went to work for the Russian anarchist Peter Lavrov, first in Germany, then in London, where he arrived in 1875 to set up the anarchist newspaper *Vperyod*. Lieberman was a spectacular failure in everything he did. He first attempted to form a union of Jewish tailors in Whitechapel but was physically attacked and assaulted by members of the Jewish establishment, who accused him (very unfairly since he was an atheist) of being a Christian missionary; the union collapsed at birth. Lieberman's newspaper was equally disastrous. While in Poland he had become convinced that Yiddish was the 'language of slaves' and that Hebrew was the appropriate language for Jews. He planned to publish a weekly Hebrew newspaper for the Jews of East London. Laudable though this might have been, it was a sure-fire failure: very few people had sufficient Hebrew to read a newspaper.

It is Lieberman's next and final scheme that commands the attention of history. On 20 May 1876, at his rooms at 40 Gun Street, Spitalfields, Lieberman founded the Hebrew Socialist Union. It was a disaster, a maximum attendance of twelve was achieved in the four meetings the union is known to have held. But, the minutes of the first meeting show that one of the constitutional aims was the foundation of a separate nation state for the Jews. This is the first historically recorded discusssion of such an aim and precedes the foundation of the World Zionist Federation by more than twenty years. Aaron and his comrades were not thinking of Palestine, or even Uganda (as Theodor Herzl and his colleagues later would); they were hoping to establish the Jewish state in Argentina, which at that time was eager to attract *émigrés* to the point of leasing them semi-autonomous tracts of land.

But Lieberman did not found a Jewish state, his organization was in disarray and there was dissension amongst the comrades. He fell in love with the wife of one of his comrades, declared his love for her and she, to avoid him, fled to New York. Lieberman pursued her, again declared his love, was again rejected, and finally blew his brains out in a hotel room in Syracuse, New York, in November 1880.

In 1884, Morris Winchevsky, a disciple of Lieberman could find no trace left of the Hebrew Socialist Union, such was the fluid nature of the ghetto population and its politics.

Winchevsky set up his own Yiddish anarchist paper *Polisher Yidl* (The Little Polish Jew), which changed its name to *Arbeiter Fraint* (The Workers' Friend) in 1885. Winchevsky's writings about the condition and exploitation of the immigrants in Whitechapel are a very useful source for the history of this area. That year (1885) Rudolf Rocker arrived in London. Rocker, a Roman Catholic by birth, came from Germany and was an anarchist. He had worked with Jews in Paris, where they were relatively prosperous, and was deeply shocked at the conditions he found in the East End. Rocker taught himself Yiddish and took over the editorship of *Arbeiter Fraint* when Winchevsky left for New York (where he would go on to found the newspaper *Vorwarts* [Forward] in 1897). Rocker lived in St Dunstan's Buildings, Stepney Way, with a Jewish anarchist commune of 'chavarim' (comrades) who worshipped the very ground on which he stood. An energetic man, Rocker next founded the International Workers' Educational Club in Berners Street (now Henriques Street) off the Commercial Road. Here, at the club which everybody called the 'Anarchist Club', Rocker organized lectures by such socialist and anarchist superstars as Prince Peter Kropotkin, William Morris, Enrico Malatesta and Louise Michel. There was a tea room (selling Russian tea) and a library, and Rocker would also organize children's trips to Hampstead Heath or lecture tours of the British Museum. In 1906 Rocker and a German Jewish anarchist called Wolf Wess successfully undertook the organization of the Jewish Tailors Union of East London, which would eventually become the modern Tailor and Garment Workers Union.

Whitechapel was becoming an amazing mixture of diversely motivated activists. The street itself had become a sort of open air labour exchange for the Jewish tailors who would line the sidewalk each day to await prospective employers. Further along Whitechapel towards the London Hospital stood the social service headquarters of the Salvation Army, which had been founded by William Booth's first sermon on Mile End Waste in 1865. The Army band would march around Whitechapel, playing outside the pubs they so deeply disapproved of and attempting to sell their paper *War Cry* to befuddled drinkers. Further along, on Mile End Road, Frederick Charrington (heir to the great Charrington Brewery) had established his National Temperance Hall and Band of Hope. Charrington could be found on a soapbox outside pubs owned by his family denouncing the evils of drink.

Back along Whitechapel, nearer to Aldgate, Canon Samuel Barnett had founded the University Settlement on Commercial Street in 1882. The Settlement, which changed its name to Toynbee Hall in the first year of operation, ran lectures on social topics: its volunteers carried out the research for Charles Booth's *London Life and Labour*. Barnett founded the Whitechapel Art Gallery in 1901, where the works of Mark Gertler, the Jewish Impressionist painter of Spitalfields, were first displayed. Lectures were well attended by the locals, who came to hear such prophets as George Bernard Shaw expound their views.

Next to the art gallery, in Whitechapel Public Library, Jewish intellectuals gathered in the reference reading room to debate all day. This became the intellectual cradle for such talents as Selig Brodetsky, the mathematician; Jacob Bronowsky, the humanist; Isaac Rosenberg, the First World War poet, and Israel Zangwill, the Zionist and novelist (about whom more later).

In 1903 Whitechapel became host to the congress of the Russian Social and Democratic Labour Party, which held its conference at the Whitechapel Methodist Mission Hall. It was during the course of this congress that the rift developed in the party which would lead to the foundation of the Menshevik and Bolshevik parties. Lenin, the leader of the Bolshevik faction, is known to have addressed two public meetings (in Russian) in Whitechapel. Another socialist active in the East End at this time was Eleanor Marx, Karl Marx's daughter. In 1888, with Annie Besant, she helped organize the women who made matches at the Bryant and May factory in Bow. Many of the 'match girls' were outworkers who made and filled the matchboxes at home helped by their children. The pay was piecework and very unrewarding. The matchgirls strike led to a whole new wave of industrial trade unions. In 1889, with Will Thorne, Eleanor Marx helped organize the Gas Workers Union and win an eight-hour working day. She was elected Secretary, then President, of this almost exclusively male union.

It was not only trade unionism and socialist ideas that the immigrants were bringing with them, but Zionism as well. We have seen the secular Zionism of Lieberman, but there were many religious Zionists as well.

The early immigrants could not afford seats in the Great Synagogue, Duke's Place. And in any case, many of them were none too convinced of the Judaism of the Anglo-Jews. For example, the concept of a Chief Rabbi (the first Chief Rabbi, Solomon Hirschell of the Great Synagogue, Duke's Place, had been appointed in 1808 to preside over the three synagogues of the Ashkenazi 'United Synagogue') struck many Russian and Polish Jews as an imposition on the autonomy of their own Rabbis, and the laxity of Anglo-Jewry on questions of Kashrut and Shechita offended many. The Anglo-Jews were not Zionists, far from it; they were well assimilated into English society, leading comfortable lives and they intended that things should remain that way.

There were early separate synagogues in Royal Mint Street (1747) and there is a reference to a 'Polish' synagogue in Sun Square off Sun Yard in 1792. Another was the Cutler Street (Houndsditch) 'Polish' synagogue of 1790. The first separate development in the East End to survive until today came with the foundation of their own synagogue by the Dutch Jews of Spitalfields. This survives today in the form of the Sandys Row Synagogue (built 1883) off Middlesex Street. It grew out of a working men's chevra or friendly society, the Hevrath Menachem Avelim Hesed Ve'emeth (Society of Kindness and Truth, established by 1854), originally dedicated to providing traditional burial. The Dutch Jews were largely cigarette and cigar makers, diamond polishers, and fruit and flower traders in Spitalfields market. The society originally had offices in White's Row, later moving to Mansell Street, Stepney, then in 1867 to the Old French Chapel in Artillery Lane. In 1870 they acquired a lease on a site at Parliament Square, Spitalfields. The property was extended and rebuilt with an entrance on Sandys Row in 1883, and had a congregation of some 500.

The establishment of this synagogue was opposed by Lionel Louis Cohen, a Conservative MP and member of the United Synagogue. Cohen argued that the Jewish population of Whitechapel and Spitalfields was declining (!) and that the congregation should take up vacant seats in the 'Great'. This was rejected as they would not have been able to afford full membership and would therefore become second-class members of the synagogue.

Another early synagogue was founded in Princes Street (now Princelet Street, Spitalfields) in 1870. In 1862 Jacob Davidson had founded the Chevra Nidrath Chem (Loyal United Friends Friendly Society), whose aim was to provide a purpose-built place of worship for the members. In 1870 the chevra bought the back garden of the house at 19 Princes Street and built the United Friends Synagogue. This was the first purpose-built 'minor synagogue' in East London and is now the third oldest synagogue in England. It remained a synagogue until 1980, when the freehold was bought by the Federation of Synagogues and sold to the Spitalfields Heritage Trust, who are currently restoring the building. It is hoped that it will be opened in the spring of 1990 as a tri-cultural heritage centre, dealing with the heritage of the Huguenots (French Calvinist refugees) who first settled this area as silk weavers in the late seventeenth century, the Jewish community, and the Bangladeshis who now live here. The Bimah (the platform from which services are conducted) still stands in the synagogue, the candelabra are still suspended from the ceiling and the panels of the ladies' galleries are covered in gilt inscriptions commemorating members of the congregation who contributed to its upkeep. The Pinchas books (account books), beautifully illuminated, and the Scrolls of the Law are in Tower Hamlets Local History Library awaiting their return to their home.

We have dealt rather harshly with the host Anglo-Jewish commuity so far in this narrative. But it should be said that many of the established Jewish community extended their help to their East European brothers and sisters.

This is particularly true of the Rothschild family; there is an abiding legend that on her death bed, Baroness Charlotte de Rothschild urged her son Nathan to devote his energies to improving the housing of Jewish workers. Whether or not this was the case, Baron Nathan Meyer de Rothschild certainly did apply himself in this direction. In late 1884 he bought a plot of land from the Metropolitan Commissioners of Works for £7,000. This piece of land occupied the space between Thrawl Street, Spitalfields and Flower and Dean Street, bounded on the other sides by Brick Lane and Commercial Street.

On 9 March 1885 Nathan called a meeting at his house in St Swithun's Court in the City of London, the leading members of Anglo-Jewry being present. Nathan took the chair, Lionel Cohen (President of the Board of Guardians), Frederick D Mocatta, Claude Montefiore, Samuel Montagu (MP for Whitechapel) and N S Joseph were present along with fourteen others. They founded the 'Four Per Cent Industrial Dwellings Company' with a capital of £40,000. The company was to have 1,600 £25 shares producing an annual dividend of 4 per cent on the capital investment. Baron Rothschild put up £10,000 plus the land he had bought for £7,000 as a gift. A loan of £8,000 was made by the Jewish Free School. In 1886 work on Charlotte de Rothschild's Dwellings began. These buildings, vast barrack-like blocks occupying the area now covered by the Toynbee Housing Association's Flower and Dean Estate, housed nearly 5,000 people. The Dwellings lasted right through until the 1980s. When they were due for demolition, a local council official called Jerry White was appointed to supervise the evacuation and rehousing of the remaining residents. Jerry became fascinated with the history of the buildings and interviewed everyone he could about their history. His book *Charlotte de Rothschild's Dwellings* is one of the best oral history sources we have for this area.

From Jerry White we learn that the Wesker family, with

Sarah Wesker leading a trousermakers' strike, lived in the Dwellings. So too did Morris Mindel and his son Mick Mindel who, at the age of twenty-eight was elected President of the United Ladies Tailor Trade Union. Chaim Zundel Maccoby, 'The Kamenitzer Maggid' lived in an apartment at 99 Rothschild's Dwellings. The Maggid was a sort of roving amateur Rabbi; originally the orator of a group in Poland known as the Lovers of Zion, he preached as the spirit moved him. A simple man, he was a strict vegetarian and never wore any garment made of a slaughtered animal. When the Maggid preached at the Great Synagogue, Spitalfields, more than 15,000 people turned out to hear him and they had to be admitted in stages through the day.

But the most illustrious son of Charlotte de Rothschild's Dwellings must be Abraham Saperstein. He was born in the Dwellings in 1908 and emigrated to the United States in the 1920s, where he founded the Harlem Globe Trotters basketball team. It is ironic that the estate that now occupies the site of Rothschild's Dwellings is covered in signs stating 'No Ball Games Allowed'. What did Abe do wrong?

By the early 1890s there were shuls (synagogues), chevrot (clubs and societies) steiblech (makeshift places of worship) all over the Spitalfields, Whitechapel, St George's area. There are records of shuls in Artillery Lane (Sandys Row), Duke's Place, Fournier Street (the Great Synagogue, Spitalfields) Goulston Street, Hanbury Street, New Court, Fashion Street, Old Castle Street, Old Montague Street, Pelham Street, Princelet Street (United Friends), Spital Square, Union Street and White's Row. In Thrawl Street, off Brick Lane, was the Etz Chaim Yeshiva (Tree of Life) Rabbinical Seminary.

There were chevrot everywhere. In 1898 the Chevra Mikra is recorded at 46 New Court, Fashion Street. In 1894 the delightfully named Society for Chanting Psalms and Visiting the Sick is registered at 113 Old Castle Street. Even better is the chevra (without known address) called the Society For Giving Alms to the Poor To Avoid An Evil Death Society.

The United Friends had established their synagogue in 1870, but it was very small. So too was the Sandys Row shul.

There were increasing numbers who could not be accommo-
dated in the existing shuls and who were not satisfied with the
makeshift arrangements of the shopfront steiblech. In 1891
Rabbi Aba Werner and friends established a congregation
known as Machzike Hadath (The Upholders of Religion).
Machzike had come into existence for two reasons: to
combat the perceived laxity of Anglo-Jewry, and to combat
the activities of organizations such as the London Society for
the Promotion of Christianity Amongst the Jews.

The London Society, with its school in Palestine Place and
its propagandist journals, had not disappeared. In 1801 the
society acquired the leasehold on the old Huguenot Chapel
'La Neuve Eglise' (built 1743) on the corner of Fournier Street
and Brick Lane. For the next ninety-one years it attempted the
conversion of the Jews. There were many other such
societies. The last was operating as recently as 1980 in
Whitechapel and was known as the Hebrew Christian
Testimony to Israel (slogan 'Hear Ye the Word of the Lord').
These societies became a joke amongst the *émigré* community. They offered grants of £50 or so to converts to settle in
Christian districts. The joke was that there were certain
unscrupulous perpetual converts, going from one society to
another constantly experiencing a change of faith! The
London Society appear to have been aware of this. In their
final report of 1892, they admitted to having spent thousands
of pounds on conversion but could only safely claim sixteen
successes. They were certain about the sixteen because they
had sent them to China as Christian Missionaries. I have
recently discovered that there is a Jewish community in
China, and one can't help wondering. . . .

The final indignity for the London Society occurred in 1892
when their recently-vacated premises became a synagogue. It
was acquired by Machzike Hadath and so became the Great
Synagogue, Spitalfields, or the Great Synagogue, Fournier
Street. As Lord Jakobovits (former Chief Rabbi) has said,
Machzike became a 'Torah fortress in Anglo-Jewry'. Rabbis
here over the years included not only the founder, Rabbi Aba
Werner, but Rabbi Al Kook (later Chief Rabbi of Israel), Rabbi

Ygael Abramsky and Rabbi Simcha Lopian. Machzike began to look for new premises in 1948, following the congregation in their move out of the East End, but the building remained a synagogue until 1965. In 1982 Machzike consecrated a new synagogue in Highfield Road, Golders Green. The old synagogue remained empty and derelict for a few years and then became a mosque to serve the new community of Bangladeshis living in the area. This building, now a listed historic monument, more than any other in the district has reflected the changing nature of the community over the centuries.

We have dealt, so far, with the political and religious life of the Jewish community of the East End, but life is not circumscribed within these limits. There was a great deal more going on. On the cultural level there was the theatre, for example. The first known Jewish dramatic society in the East End was the Hebrew Amateur Society founded at the corner of Princelet Street and Wilkes Street in 1882. Tragically the building burned down in 1892, killing eleven members of the company, but fortunately for the theatre world, the leading actor was absent that evening – Jacob Adler would go on to a great career on the stage in the United States, where his granddaughter, Stella, still follows in his footsteps today.

There were Yiddish theatres in Whitechapel and Commercial Road. They gave pleasure and relaxation to the local community and a first step on the ladder to many actors who later would perform on a wider stage. The Pavilion Theatre in Whitechapel was still performing Yiddish plays as late as 1965, but sadly the building was later declared an unsafe structure and is now gone. Another Yiddish theatre on Commercial Road and Cannon Street Road has now become the Palaseum Gujarati Cinema.

Literature, too, was being produced in the area. Fashion Street is remarkable for its literary history. This little road, only one hundred yards long and full of tailoring sweatshops, has been home over the years to Israel Zangwill, Jack London, Arnold Wesker and Wolf Mankowitz. Zangwill grew up on Fashion Street, and in 1892, while working as a teacher

at the Jewish Free School, he published his first novel
Children of the Ghetto. Much of the action in the novel takes
place on Fashion Street and in nearby Brick Lane. Zangwill
won a literary prize for his novel, but was also summoned in
front of Dr Abrahams the Headmaster of the JFS and Lord
Rothschild the Governor and told 'change your style or resign
from this school'. Zangwill's offence had been to reproduce
phonetically the accents of the East End. The JFS was in the
business of moulding respectable English girls and boys and
wanted no such reminders of the ethnic past. Zangwill
resigned but went on to become the first Secretary of the
World Zionist Federation.

Jack London was already a world-famous novelist when he
came to Fashion Street in 1902. He had come to England for
the coronation of King Edward VII. In his book *People of the
Abyss*, London tells us he had attended the coronation in the
morning and that night was walking along the Embankment
by the riverside. He was shocked to discover people sleeping
on benches on the Embankment, and contrasted this hidden
poverty with the immense wealth and power he had seen on
display at the coronation. He decided to experience poverty
at first hand. He went to Thomas Cook's travel agency and
asked for a guide to the East End. Cook's told him that they
could supply a guide to India or Africa, but not to the East
End. So he made his own way to the East End and took
lodgings in Fashion Street. After a few weeks he moved out to
sleep rough in the parks and graveyards of the district.
Zangwill and London are probably the best guides to the
nature and feeling of this area at the turn of the century.

In the inter-war years Fashion Street was the childhood
home of playwright Arnold Wesker and Wolf Mankowitz,
who now writes screenplays in Hollywood. In 1951, Mankowitz published a children's novel entitled *A Kid For Two
Farthings*. It is the delightful story of a boy called Joe whose
mother has been abandoned by her husband. Joe and his
mother live on Fashion Street with Kandinsky, a tailor and
storyteller. Kandinsky tells Joe that his father has gone to
Africa to get him a unicorn, and eventually Kandinsky buys

Joe a kid in Petticoat Lane (Middlesex Street) Market. Joe spends the rest of the story waiting for the goat to grow a horn and become a unicorn. *A Kid For Two Farthings* was made into a film in 1954 starring David Kossoff as Kandinsky, and was the last of the Jewish East End Films.

Through much of its recent history nobody in their right mind would have chosen to remain in the Spitalfields/ Whitechapel area, and as early as 1900 (when the Jewish population was at its height) the local community was talking of 'the North-West Passage' – i.e. people were moving out in an arc to the north and west of London; to Dalston, Stamford Hill, Golders Green, Hendon, Finchley, Edgware. It is here that the active Jewish communities can be found today.

Much had been done to encourage this movement and the cultural assimilation that accompanied it. The Board of Guardians of the Jewish Poor (operating from its headquarters in Middlesex Street), as we have seen, did not encourage East Europeans to come to England in the first place. But, once they had arrived, the Board shouldered its responsibilities. Between 1900 and 1910 it made 26,479 loans to the East End's Jews, averaging £7.00 per loan. The loans were interest free and repayable at six pence in the pound per week. They were made to people who wished to set up as independent traders or as their own masters.

Lord Rothschild's charity, 'The Four Per Cent', was also involved in social engineering. Having built Charlotte de Rothschild's Dwellings the company built no more housing in this area. In 1904 the Four Per Cent opened their new blocks, called Navarino Mansions, in Dalston Lane, Hackney. In 1905 estates were built in Camberwell, South London and Stoke Newington: dispersion would lead to assimilation.

Little remains of the old ghetto today. A walk around the area will produce a host of Jewish business names: Schloss Woollens on Goulston Street, Ginsberg's Travel Goods and Marks' Delicatessen in Wentworth Street, Mendel's Shoes on Bell Lane, the remarkable Baum's Polish Vodka Shop (twenty or more varieties of vodka plus Israeli kosher wine and Passover slivovitz) on Toynbee Street; the Sephardi banana merchants David Kira on Fournier Street and Verde on Brushfield Street; Gale's Furs on Fournier Street, Rozansky's and Wolman's on Brick Lane, Ivor Dembina Hosiery on Wilkes Street, Minsky's Textiles on Fashion Street (inhabited by the ebullient Mr Minsky, ever willing to pass the time of day in Yiddish with the overseas visitor); Elfe's Monumental Mason's on Brick Lane.

On Whitechapel is Bloom's Kosher Restaurant proclaiming itself 'the Most Famous Kosher Restaurant in Great Britain' (which it is). You can get a good salt beef on rye sandwich and lemon tea (at a price) in Bloom's and their sit-down meals are often good. Their waiters have, as they diplomatically put it, 'character'. More homely, and cheaper, is the Kosher Luncheon Club at Morris Kasler Hall, Greatorex Street, off Whitechapel. This club, with its 'regulars', is open Monday to Friday 12–3 pm. It's worth the stroll down Whitechapel as far as the club, if only to look at the Old Whitechapel Bell Foundry along the way (where the Liberty Bell was cast and exported without intent!) and the new mosque on Whitechapel, a sign of how times have changed in this most fascinating corner of London.

Jack the Ripper's East End

1 Working Lads' Institute. Several of the Ripper inquests were held here.

2 Durward Street (at the junction with Winthrop Street) was formerly Buck's Row, scene of the first murder – Mary Ann Nichols.

3 Henriques Street (formerly Berners Street). Scene of the third murder – Elizabeth Stride.

4 Modern **Mulberry Street** was formerly Sion Square, where Aaron Kozminski lived. Between Plumber's Row and Adler Street was a street, now entirely demolished, called Mulberry Street. This was where John Pizer lived.

5 Hanbury Street. Scene of the second murder – Annie Chapman.

6 Corner of Commercial Street and Fournier Street. **The Ten Bells pub**, a haunt of Ripperologists.

7 Dorset Street, now demolished, was about here. Scene of the fifth and final murder – Mary Kelly.

8 City Darts pub. Formerly the Princess Alice, the early suspect 'Leather Apron' was reported to drink here.

9 Goulston Street. A bloodstained piece of Eddowes' apron was found here. Dropped by Jack the Ripper as he fled the murder scene, it suggests the direction in which he was heading.

10 Mitre Square. Scene of the fourth murder – Katherine Eddowes.

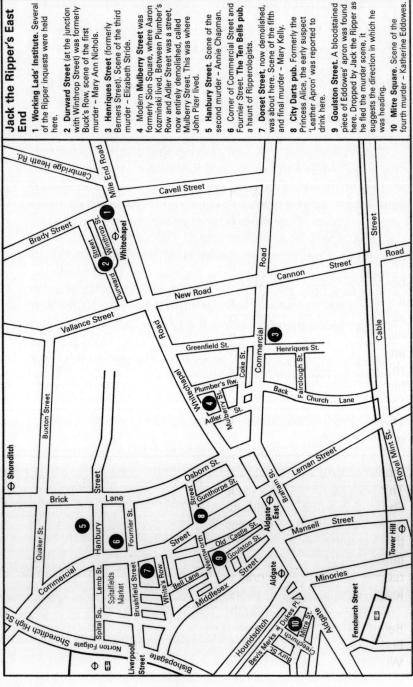

JACK THE RIPPER'S EAST END
Martin Fido

The East End is historic criminal territory. Dick Turpin was born in Whitechapel and apprenticed to a butcher there. And it was in Whitechapel that he accidentally shot his confederate, Tom King, when escaping from the constables. Bill Sikes was placed in Bethnal Green lodgings by Dickens: his girlfriend, the prostitute Nancy, came from Shadwell. Fagin shifted his den to Whitechapel when Mr Brownlow scared him out of the Saffron Hill area. Ikey Solomons, 'the Prince of Fences', operated from Gravel Lane, off Petticoat Lane, in the 1820s. He is sometimes (wrongly) identified as Fagin's real-life original.

Gangs of muggers and protection racketeers infested the region, from the Hoxton Hi-Rips and Limehouse Forty Thieves of Victoria's reign to the twentieth-century Shoreditch and Spitalfields gangs headed by Darkie the Coon (who was really a Jew named Bogart) and Arthur Harding of the Vendetta Mob. Steinie Morrison, the Stepney burglar, fenced his stolen wares through Leon Beron, bagman for a big receiving operation conducted from The Three Tuns pub in Jewry Street in the early years of this century.

Closer to our own time, the Kray twins were brought up in Bethnal Green and opened their serious operations in Mile End. Tommy 'Scarface' Smithson's murderer lived in Whitechapel and Spitalfields. Ginger Marks was taken for a

ride in Cheshire Street while masterminding a break-in on the
Bethnal Green Road. The Pen Club murder – a lethal
gangland brawl of the 1960s – took place in the last surviving
part of wicked old Dorset Street.

Famous Whitechapel murders include Wainwright's dis-
memberment, burial and exhumation of his mistress in Vine
Court (he was subsequently arrested while driving her from
Whitechapel High Street to the Borough, wrapped up in
malodorous parcels). Steinie Morrison seems to have fingered
Leon Beron in the Whitechapel and Stepney streets during the
early midnight hours before the little fence's body was found
with a mutilated face on Clapham Common. Ronnie Kray
shot George Cornell in the Blind Beggar close to Whitechapel
underground station, on the edge of Bethnal Green.

Yet there is only one man instantly recognized as 'The
Whitechapel Murderer': only one set of crimes catalogued in
library files as 'The Whitechapel Murders': only one
Whitechapel murderer who has ever had a pub named after
him: Jack the Ripper.

Funny that he should be 'The Whitechapel Murderer', in a
way. Of the five women he probably killed, only two died in
Whitechapel, and one of those was on its border with St
George's in the East. Of the remaining three, two were killed
in Spitalfields, and one just inside the City of London.

And it was a site in the City that really gave the East End its
most famous murders: the church of St Botolph-without-
Aldgate.

The pavement surrounding that splendid Wren church was
the location of an unwritten agreement between the police
and local prostitutes. As long as the ladies walked round and
round the church, they would not be arrested for soliciting or
obstruction. This made the church one of the great 'beats' of
the late nineteenth century, and at one time or other,
practically every prostitute working in the East End stayed in
the common lodging houses which packed three of the roads
running off Commercial Street, to the north-east of the
church.

Flower and Dean Street, Thrawl Street and Dorset Street

were the last streets in the area to remain in Gentile hands as a flood of Jewish immigration filled the district in the wake of Russian pogroms and Bismarck's clearance of Silesia. G R Sims, the journalist who wrote 'Christmas Day in the Workhouse', described the three streets as little Gentile oases in a Yiddish-speaking town of about a square mile. He also noted that they were the great centres of vice and crime. The Reverend Samuel Barnett, vicar of St Jude's, called them 'the wicked quarter-mile'.

It cost 4d (approximately one pound at today's values) for a night shared with a stranger in a verminous bed in one of the wicked quarter-mile's doss-houses. The beds were packed six or seven to a room. The more reputable houses would not allow people of opposite gender to share beds; the more free-and-easy didn't care who slept with whom.

But basically the ladies of the East End pavements had no homes or rooms of their own. Their charge for their services was normally 4d, so they had to have more clients than they could take to their rented beds in even the most liberal lodging houses if they were to eat as well as sleep. Or drink: an activity most of them took at least as seriously as eating.

So their practice was to take clients into the back alleys and enclosed yards, or under the dark railway arches which packed the district. One railway arch off the Minories (near the City of London Polytechnic today) was the site of mad German hairdresser Charles Ludwig's tentative assault on Elizabeth Burns during the Ripper scare. The police thought they'd got their murderer until the Ripper struck again, twice in one night, while Ludwig was safe in a cell on remand.

Another old railway arch in Pinchin Street, off Back Church Lane, yielded a woman's headless and legless torso in 1889: almost certainly a companion crime to the unsolved 'Whitehall torso murder', when the cheeky villain actually dumped most of his victim's remains in the foundations of New Scotland Yard as they were being dug. It started a brief revival of the Ripper scare, but was not really connected with his activities.

East End prostitutes were perfect targets for a serial

murderer. As a matter of professional skill, they knew places where the policemen on beat duty would not disturb them for ten or fifteen minutes. Time for hurried coupling. Time for a client who was not quite what he seemed to cut their throats and hastily mutilate their abdomens.

Curiously, this sordid outdoor prostitution has survived, though common lodging houses no longer exist for Spitalfields' ladies of the night. When the BBC devoted a *Timewatch* programme to the Ripper to mark the centenary of his murders, producer John Triffit managed to interview some of the women who still make their living on the pavements of Commercial Street and Brick Lane. He discovered that they still take clients to corners in the open air. But they have learned from the fate of their predecessors: they are no longer so discreetly secretive. 'We do it as near to the pavement as we can,' one told him. 'We'd do it in the middle of the road if the punters would let us. It's safer.'

Polly Nichols, the first Ripper victim, died while using a site that even today's prostitutes might feel was pretty safe. You won't find Buck's Row in an *A to Z*. It was a narrow, but fairly reputable street behind Whitechapel Road, close to where the underground station stands today. A row of recently-built terraced cottages graced its south side in 1888, with a yard-gate between the eastern end and a huge grim Board School. The north side of the street was lined with warehouses locally called 'wharves' as there had once been a canal where the railway tracks to Bethnal Green now run.

Polly Nichols was thrown out of her doss-house in Thrawl Street at half-past one in the morning for not having the money to pay her rent. She was confident that she would be back. 'I'll soon get my doss money,' she said. 'See what a jolly bonnet I've got now.' Considering that the fashionable bonnets and shawls of the period gave women the outfit we would associate with Toad's washerwoman, it might seem that Polly was optimistic in thinking that she presented an erotically alluring appearance. But no doubt the Old Mother Riley rig was not unappealing to those who had only seen it on younger women.

Polly had been drinking in the Frying Pan in Brick Lane earlier that evening, and she was wandering uncertainly away from it again when her friend Nelly Holland encountered her in Osborn Street at 2.00am. Nelly urged her to come home to the doss-house. Polly refused, saying she had earned her money three times over that night and drunk it away, and now she was off to earn it again.

She went to earn it in the apparently safe situation of the open gateway between the houses and the school in Buck's Row. Mrs Emma Green's bedroom directly overlooked the gateway on the same side of the road. Mr and Mrs Walter Purkess lived in the manager's house attached to Essex Wharf, immediately opposite the gate. And around 3.15am, the little narrow street was very heavily policed. PC John Thain walked past its eastern end and looked down it. PC John Neil came along the parallel Winthrop Street and then walked the length of Buck's Row. Sergeant Kerby came along it at the same time. None saw anything out of the ordinary.

But twenty-five minutes later, carter Charles Cross, on his way to work, spotted a heap in the gateway which he took to be a tarpaulin. Going over to examine it, he found Polly Nichols with her skirt pulled up. He was soon joined by another carter named Robert Paul, who pulled the skirt down. Neither of them saw that her throat had been cut back to the spine. Nobody realized until much later that day that under her skirt a great gash ran down her abdomen, leaving her intestines slightly protruding. The two carters hurried off to find a policeman, and the great Jack the Ripper scare was under way.

So was the campaign to erase the name Buck's Row from the street directories. It is said that the inhabitants objected to a jocular postman who passed from house to house, saying, 'Number 5 Murder Row, I believe'. Within six weeks they had petitioned for the name to be changed, and ever since then it has been Durward Street.

The Buck's Row murder gave rise to several of the legends that have attached to the Ripper ever since. Neither Mrs Green, who said she was a light sleeper, nor Mrs Purkess, who said she was actually awake and walking up and down her bedroom most of the night, heard a sound from the street until the police began calling for assistance. It was suggested that the murderer was very silent, and crept up on his prey wearing rubber-soled boots. These long had a slightly sinister reputation as unduly secretive footwear (compared with leather or hobnails), and individual policemen during the Ripper investigation tied strips of rubber under their soles in the hope that they might come silently upon the murderer.

In Brady Street, at the eastern end of Buck's Row, Mrs Sarah Colwell fuelled this legend of unusual silence. She claimed to have heard a woman running and screaming as if she was being struck during the night. Yet Mrs Colwell could hear no pursuer's footsteps.

In the morning, Mrs Colwell and some newspapermen thought they could discern traces of blood in Brady Street. They wondered whether Polly had been killed there, and then carried down the street to the gutter where she was found. After all, Dr Llewellyn, who certified the death, reported that there was only 'a wine-glass-and-a-half-full of blood in the gutter'. But Inspector Helson told Polly's inquest where the rest went. It had soaked into her hair, her ulster, her dress, her stays. She had definitely died where she was found.

There were more drops of blood at the other end of Buck's Row, where it broadens out into a space under the Board School which served as the Hyde Park of the Left in Victorian East London. William Morris and Bernard Shaw spoke there from soap-boxes, and mass meetings supported the great dock strikes of 1889 and 1911.

The newspapers believed the blood had dripped from the murderer's weapon. The police were doubtful. And since three slaughtermen who had been working all night in Winthrop Street had rushed around to see the body at 5.00am, it may just as easily have dripped off their aprons and knives. There were few ways of distinguishing human from other mammalian blood in 1888.

Another legend stemming in part from this murder was that

the Ripper had an extraordinary and unusual knowledge of the warren of back streets and alleys in the East End, since he escaped unseen by Sergeant Kerby, Constables Neil and Thain, and Constable Mizen who was fetched by Cross and Paul. In fact, since Cross and Paul found Mizen in Hanbury Street some way off to the west, there were seven different routes the murderer might have taken to the south or west which would have led him well out of Mizen's way. There can be little doubt that he knew the district, and pretty certainly lived in it. But his knowledge was not really extraordinary.

Though this was the first Ripper murder, the scare began at once. For the newspapers instantly ascribed to the same hand two previous killings in that same year of Whitechapel prostitutes who had been abdominally injured. The earlier, on 3 April, undoubtedly had nothing to do with the Ripper. Emma Smith had been attacked at midnight on the crossroads formed by Osborn Street, Brick Lane, Wentworth Street and Old Montague Street. Four youths who had followed her from Whitechapel High Street robbed her, raped her, and thrust something like a blunt stick into her. Though she passed into a coma and died in the London Hospital four days later, she remained conscious long enough to say positively that she had been attacked by a gang of sadistic muggers, not a lone maniac.

The other murder victim wrongly ascribed to the Ripper was killed early in August. Martha Tabram or Turner was savagely stabbed to death in a tenement building at the top of George Yard.

Today the lane is named Gunthorpe Street: a narrow, bending cobbled alley with some old industrial buildings on one side, and a picturesque arch leading out to Whitechapel High Street at the bottom end. Under the arch lies the side door to the White Hart, a pub which was not only standing in the Ripper's day, but whose basement housed Inspector Frederick Abberline's suspect.

Abberline was sent from Scotland Yard to co-ordinate the detectives on the ground. He was not, as so many people

wrongly believe, in charge of the case. He was not even
shown the medical reports on the victims. But in 1902 after
his retirement he did reach a conclusion as to the Ripper's
identity, as he told the *Pall Mall Gazette* in two interviews the
following April.

In 1888 there was a barber's shop in the basement of the
White Hart. It employed a twenty-three year old Pole called
Severin Klosowski. Some years after the murders he went to
America and changed his name to George Chapman. He
came back to England late in the 1890s, and set up as a
publican. He remained intensely pro-American, and preferred to call any bar where he served 'the American bar'. He
was also something of a womanizer. He was living with a Mrs
Shadrach Spink when he opened his first pub. When she
died, he moved to the Borough of Southwark, opened
another pub in Union Street, and took another woman as his
common law wife.

Then he had a run of bad luck. His woman died. His pub
burned down. And the insurance company refused to pay his
claim. They accused him of arson. Undaunted, he took a new
pub in the Borough High Street, and persuaded his eighteen
year old barmaid, Maud Marsh, to live with him as his wife.
Before the year was out, she too had died.

The doctor refused to sign her death certificate. Two wives
dying suddenly in the space of twenty months seemed
suspicious. Maud Marsh proved to be full of tartar emetic. So,
when they had been exhumed, did Chapman's previous two
wives. Evidently he was one of those unduly tender-minded
men who can't bear to hurt a woman by saying, 'I'm sorry,
darling, it's all over.' Instead, he spared them the pain and
himself a quarrel by feeding them tartar emetic.

Abberline went to his trial, and on learning that George
Chapman was really a Pole named Klosowski who had been
living in Whitechapel in 1888, he is alleged to have said to
the arresting officer, Inspector Godley, 'I see you've got Jack
the Ripper at last.'

He explained in more detail to the *Pall Mall Gazette*. He
told the paper that the police knew the motive for the

murders: they were to extract the victims' wombs for sale to an American doctor who was writing a treatise on the uterus and offering high prices for specimens. Abberline noted that Chapman, as a Polish-trained barber-surgeon, would know how to locate and remove the womb. He added that he had an obvious connection with America. And for good measure threw in the suggestions that Martha Tabram, found dead in the lane where Klosowski worked, was really the first Ripper victim, and that it would pretty certainly be found that similar serial murders had occurred in America while Chapman was over there.

Unfortunately, Abberline was quite wrong. Martha was most likely not a Ripper victim. Subsequent research has established that there were no outbreaks of serial murder in the parts of America where Klosowski lived as Chapman. And the motive Abberline postulated had been proposed by the coroner at the second Ripper victim's inquest and widely publicized. But the coroner himself silently dropped the theory when the *British Medical Journal* pointed out that the doctor in question had left Britain eighteen months before the murders started, and had never paid anyone high prices for specimens: he had been given all he needed by hospitals, as a reputable researcher.

Moreover, Abberline was evidently unaware that the Ripper's last victim had her womb extracted but not removed from the scene of the crime. It remained on her bed with her body.

All Abberline's theory really tells us is that he actually knew surprisingly little about the facts of the case.

The second genuine Ripper murder took place in Hanbury Street, part of which still looks much as it did 100 years ago: a fairly narrow street of grimy four-storey houses, many of them with flat shop fronts. But No 29, where the Ripper killed Annie Chapman, has been replaced by a brewery building.

It is one of London's most haunted buildings. Invisible from the road, the old backyard step of No 29 remains inside the brewery yard. At 4.50am on 8 September 1888, a local resident, John Richardson, sat on that step and looked at the empty backyard before him as he trimmed a piece of loose leather off his boot. One hour later another resident, John Davis, came down into the yard and found Annie Chapman lying alongside the fence with her head almost touching the step. Her throat had been cut. Her abdomen had been savagely mutilated.

Ever since, local people have reported seeing her ghost hanging around the step. But in the brewery building she now has more company than she did when Hanbury Street was a row of shops and houses. Ghosts of monks and nuns are seen in parts of the building where an old monastery and a convent once stood. And the boardroom strikes deathly cold to the psychic, no matter what the thermometer reads.

Annie Chapman's body was examined by police surgeon Bagster Phillips, and he is responsible for our image of the Ripper as a man in a top hat and dark cape, carrying a black bag. For Phillips believed that the mutilations were the work of an expert, and his conclusion that Jack was Dr Jack gained wide currency.

Far less publicity was given to the views of the other doctors involved in the case. Five of them concurred that the murderer had no skill at all, not even the skill of a butcher. The sixth, with some apparent self-contradiction, suggested that he knew the location of organs in the body.

Serious Ripper historians today do not believe that Jack was a doctor, though dabblers still put forward such exploded ideas as the complicity of Sir William Gull, physician-in-ordinary to the Queen, in a Masonic conspiracy to kill prostitutes who were blackmailing the royal family; or that the Tsarist police deliberately shipped a dangerous sex maniac named Alexander Pedachenko into London in order to discredit the Metropolitan Police whom they blamed for tolerating the Russian dissidents enjoying political asylum in the East End. Both these stories are total fabrications. The painter Joseph Gorman Sickert has confessed that he made up the first: the second has been shown by writer Melvin Harris to be Bolshevik disinformation aimed at tarnishing the reputation of Tsarists.

Yet more colourful is the case against himself manufactured by Robert Donston Stevenson who called himself Dr Rosslyn D'Onston and dabbled in black magic and freelance journalism at the time of the murders. He realized, subsequently, that there was prestige to be gained in black magic circles by letting people believe they had 'found out' he was the Ripper, and he persuaded two silly women and Melvin Harris that he was. According to Stevenson's fantasy, the aim of the murders was a ritual which would give the killer the gift of invisibility, and he stole the missing organs hidden under his neckties. Unfortunately, neither he nor the infamous occultist Aleister Crowley, who gave enthusiastic currency to Stevenson's claim, knew enough about the murders to know how many victims had organs taken from them, or what pattern the disembowelled victims formed on a map of the streets.

Oddly enough, though, the names of two Russian doctors *were* in the hands of Scotland Yard at or after the time of the murders. The name of Dr Michael Ostrog appears in a long set of notes on the case drafted by Melville Macnaghten, Chief Constable of the Metropolitan CID, in 1894, as the last of three suspects he had heard about. And the name of Dr Konovalov crops up in a letter from a senior Scotland Yard policeman of the next generation, who attributes the belief that Konovalov was the Ripper to the French Police.

Hitherto, both these men have seemed impossible to trace. But now investigator Nick Warren, a surgeon from Uxbridge, has found an Okhrana (Tsarist secret police) document which actually does contain a report from Paris on Konovalov, and two other researchers have traced Ostrog. Ripper enthusiasts look forward to forthcoming publication of the details on these men.

Annie Chapman's murder initiated another of the great legends of the Ripper, to the effect that he piled her coins and rings ritually at her feet. This is quite untrue: a story which has grown up through repetitions and exaggerations of an original press error. In fact, Annie's two brass rings were missing from her hand, and the police were anxious to find them, as they had probably been stolen by her murderer.

A more significant press story concerned the hunt for 'Leather Apron'. A leather apron was found beside Annie's body. It had nothing to do with the murder, being the property of the landlady's son at 29 Hanbury Street, and left out in the yard after normal washing. But it prompted a sensational hullabaloo in the newspapers.

It was already known that the Metropolitan Police's principal suspect was a poor East End Jew nicknamed 'Leather Apron'. Prostitutes had told the detectives that this man habitually threatened and abused them on the streets, sometimes with a knife, and sometimes saying, 'I'll rip you up.' They were sure he was mad, expected him to go over the top, and believed he had now done so and started committing the murders.

Unfortunately they did not know his name or address: only that he lived somewhere near Plumber's Row and Buck's Row, and that he drank at the Princess Alice on the corner of Commercial Street and Wentworth Street. (The same pub is today called the City Darts, and its landlord will happily explain its Ripper connections to visitors.) He hung around the doss-houses, and was known by sight to men attached to Crossingham's lodging house in Dorset Street. He sometimes wore a deerstalker cap, like a man seen talking to Annie Chapman on the Hanbury Street footpath some half an hour or more before Davis found the body. And he sometimes wore his leather apron on the streets. Hence his nickname among the prostitutes. Hence, too, the probability that he was either a butcher, a carpenter or a shoemaker.

With the discovery of the apron in the yard of 29 Hanbury Street, the press went wild with stories about 'Leather Apron', the murderous Jewish immigrant. And in the East End this uproar nearly prompted race riots. People started beating up Jews on the streets, saying, 'No Englishman would commit murders like this.' The police had to act fast and firmly to quash the 'Leather Apron' scare: race riots could have cost far more life than a single obsessed maniac.

Two days after Annie Chapman's death, Sergeant William

Thick went to 22 Mulberry Street, and arrested thirty-six year old John Pizer with the words. 'You're just the man I want'. Pizer's hats and knives were taken away for examination, and he himself was paraded before a central European vagrant called Emmanuel Violenia, who claimed to have seen Annie Chapman talking to a man in Hanbury Street. Violenia immediately declared that Pizer was the man, and that he knew him as 'Leather Apron'. But when he was taken to see Annie's body in the mortuary, he started to back off, saying he wasn't certain this was the woman he had seen. The police decided he had come forward with false information out of a morbid wish to be shown the corpse. They did not use him as a witness.

But they put Pizer up at Annie Chapman's inquest, declaring that he was 'Leather Apron', and pointing out that they knew him to be completely innocent. For on the night of Polly Nichols' death he had been five miles away in Holloway, and he chatted that night to a Holloway police- man who remembered him.

Until 1987 it was generally assumed that Pizer was indeed 'Leather Apron'. Then, for the first time, it was noticed that the local papers had reported that Pizer denied it. Moreover, it became clear that two weeks after Pizer's appearance at the inquest, the police were still looking for someone who seemed very like 'Leather Apron', only with the nickname and the dangerous epithet 'Jewish' dropped. Pizer had not been arrested in an out-of-the-way hiding place, as previous writers assumed. 22 Mulberry Street had been his home since he was four years old, and for eighteen of those years, Sergeant Thick had known him.

In fact, the only evidence that Pizer was 'Leather Apron' was Sergeant Thick's claim that he himself had worked in Whitechapel for a long time and knew that everybody there always meant John Pizer when they used the nickname 'Leather Apron'. If Pizer had not been pushed out of the court by the coroner, there can be little doubt that Thick would have faced the embarrassing question, 'Why wasn't the bootmaker named and picked up sooner, thus preventing an anti-semitic panic?' Pizer seems to have been dubiously identified as 'Leather Apron', so that the heat could be taken off the Jewish community.

Three weeks after Annie Chapman's death, the Ripper struck again. Henriques Street, Whitechapel, was then called Berner Street. At its junction with Fairclough Street stood an old Board School, like the one still standing in Buck's Row. Opposite the school, on the north side of a little enclosed courtyard, was a social and political club, mainly used by local Jewish anarchists and socialists. A school stands today where the old International Workers' Educational Club once stood, and the Bernhard Baron Settlement, a large Jewish community centre, has replaced the old Board School.

At 1.00am on 30 September, the club steward, Louis Diemschütz, drove his pony and cart into the courtyard, only to find a woman lying behind the gates. He jumped to two conclusions: she must be drunk, and she was probably his wife. But he checked up in the clubroom first, and on discovering his wife upright and sober, came out to find that the woman in the yard was actually dead with her throat cut.

Her name was 'Long Liz' Stride. She was a Swedish immigrant who had married a Poplar coffee shop keeper named Stride about twelve years earlier, and drifted back into prostitution after her husband died. She had previously been familiar with the trade in Sweden, where she had left behind a bad reputation and an illegitimate baby. Berner Street, close to the parish of St George's in the East, was her stamping ground because it abutted on the old Swedish church off the Ratcliff Highway. And its pastor used to give Liz hand-outs when she fell on hard times. The books detailing charitable donations to her are still in the possession of the new Swedish church in Marylebone.

She had not been ripped. But the police put this down to her murderer being frightened off by the approach of Diemschütz's cart. They had little doubt that she was a Ripper victim, and that on being disturbed he left her body and went immediately to find someone else on whom to gratify his frustrated and perverted desire.

It is worth noting that Liz Stride was an exceedingly good looking woman with a beautiful bone structure. Too many writers erroneously describe the Ripper's victims as miserable harridans, prematurely aged by vice and gin. In fact, while all were desperately poor, two were strikingly good looking; a third looked ten years younger than her age of forty-two; and the other two were perfectly normal looking women in their forties.

Katherine Eddowes' last night on earth began with a happy round of drinks. At 8.30pm she was causing a drunken disturbance in Aldgate High Street. According to Tom Cullen, who produced the first good post-war book on the Ripper, she was imitating a fire engine, and attracted a small crowd. Certainly she then lay down on the pavement to sleep, and City Police Constable Lewis Robinson arrested her and took her off to Bishopsgate Police Station.

She was locked in a cell to sleep off her over-indulgence, and was heard to be awake and singing quietly to herself half an hour after midnight. She seems to have been a cheerful, feckless little person, rarely quarrelling, often singing, and merrily drinking away money which she scrounged shamelessly off her nearest and dearest.

Soon she called out to know when she would be released. She knew that the tolerant City Police, unlike their more austere colleagues in the Metropolitan Police, did not charge drunks who had not caused actual damage or given serious offence. The desk sergeant gave her a benign wigging for getting drunk, and with a cheery, 'Good night, old cock!' she left the police station just at the time when Elizabeth Stride's body was being found in Berner Street.

Half an hour later she was standing outside the narrow covered alley running from Duke's Place to Mitre Square, with her hand resting amiably on a young man's chest. He wore a peaked cloth cap, a pea-jacket and a red neckerchief. He had a fresh complexion and a small fair moustache, slightly turning up.

Another twenty minutes went by, and City PC Edward Watkins on beat duty came into Mitre Square at 1.50am. He found Katherine's body on the footpath outside three empty cottages in the south-west corner. Her throat had been cut. Her abdomen had been ripped open and savagely attacked. V-shaped incisions had been made in her cheeks, pointing to her eyes, and her eyelids had been nicked through. And a great slashing cut had sliced off the tip of her nose. The murders were becoming more horrible.

When the police surgeon examined the body, he found that Katherine's uterus and left kidney had been taken away. He it was who remarked, certainly correctly, that if the murderer was deliberately looking for a kidney as such, he must have had some knowledge of anatomy. For it is not easy to find a kidney from the front of the body.

Most Ripper experts, however, note the amount of random slashing which had defaced practically all the organs in the abdomen, and note, too, that the mutilations started in the genital region with the removal of the uterus – the first organ that would present itself in that area. From this it is deduced that the man was totally unskilled, as the overwhelming majority of doctors at the time agreed. The missing organs were not deliberately sought: they were randomly taken as they happened to fall to hand in the ferocious attacks.

It is interesting that the press did not report the extraction of Katherine's uterus, even though Dr Brown gave full information about it to the inquest. Her missing kidney, on the other hand, was widely reported. It seems likely that the police were practising the cautious habit of withholding a little information from the public so that a suspect under questioning might prove his guilt if he knew more than the newspapers had revealed.

The missing kidney evoked its own repercussion. Three weeks after the murder, Mr George Lusk, a stolid bowler-hatted local builder, attracted some publicity as the secretary of a Whitechapel Vigilance Committee of local businessmen. These worthies were pressing the police to offer a reward for information – something Scotland Yard was only too willing to do, but that the Home office strictly forbade. The Yard, at the same time, were pressing for Whitechapel's street-lighting to be improved, and on this point the Vigilance Committee backed the police strongly. While he was in the public eye, Mr Lusk began to fear that he and his son were being watched by a suspicious looking bearded man. He sought police protection. Soon after this had been reported, Mr Lusk received a small parcel through the post, accompanied by a crudely written mis-spelled letter datelined 'From Hell' and signed 'Catch me when you can, Mishter Lusk'. It purported to come from the murderer, and it averred that the parcel contained half of Katherine Eddowes' missing kidney in a state of preservation. The writer claimed to have fried and eaten the other half, adding, 'It was very nise'.

There was, indeed, half a kidney in the parcel.

Mr Lusk, a sensible man, concluded that the parcel was a hoax and the kidney probably a dog's. But his friends persuaded him to hand it in for medical examination, and Dr Openshaw of the London Hospital pronounced it to be human and preserved in spirits of wine.

Unfortunately, the press enlarged on Dr Openshaw's statement lavishly. He was said to have described the kidney as 'ginny' and to have identified it as coming from the body of a forty-five year old woman. Dr Openshaw issued a denial of these embroideries, and Dr Sedgwick Saunders, the City analyst, issued an acerbic statement pointing out the impossibility of identifying the sex of a kidney, and the fact that gin leaves no renal traces. He magisterially commented that students could, and often did, buy kidneys of this kind for a few pence from hospital porters and used them for practical jokes. He believed this was a student hoax, and the overwhelming majority of Ripper experts today agree with him.

He did, however, make one curious error. He declared that the kidney remaining in Katherine Eddowes' body was perfectly healthy. Since writer (and City policeman) Donald Rumbelow discovered Dr Brown's post mortem notes among the inquest papers, it has been known that this was not quite the case. Nick Warren points out that Brown uses words that could hardly be bettered as a description of symptoms of

Bright's Disease. And it has long been known that Major Smith, Acting Commissioner of the City Police at the time of the murder, recorded in his memoirs that both the kidney sent to Mr Lusk and the kidney remaining in Katherine Eddowes' body were affected with Bright's Disease. As Smith was the sole source for this claim, and he is extravagantly inaccurate in most of his stories about the Whitechapel murders, experts have long followed (author) Richard Whittington-Egan's lead in discounting the importance of the Lusk Kidney. Most still do, but Nick Warren postulates this is an area where some fruitful rethinking and research might be done.

The other famous pseudonymous correspondence made public after the night of the double murder was the letter and postcard signed 'Jack the Ripper'. It was the first appearance of this name, and it instantly took hold of the public imagination and has gripped it ever since.

The letter, posted to the Central News Agency, purported to come from the murderer and jeeringly declared his intention of returning to work soon, and of cutting off his next victim's ears for the police. The postcard, sent to the same recipient the day after the double murders, regretted not having had time to get the ears.

For many years it was believed that these communications – and even a number of the numerous obviously imitative hoaxes which succeeded them – were the work of the murderer: that he had given himself his startling name.

Richard Whittington-Egan first undermined this widespread misconception, by pointing out that the postcard had been sent *after* the double murders had been reported in the press, and not before. And since most experts have come to place far more confidence in the Scotland Yard chiefs than used to be the case, nobody seriously argues any longer that the notorious 'Ripper letters' were the murderer's handiwork. For two successive heads of the CID, and one distinguished Chief Inspector, all separately recorded their certainty that the postcard and letter were forged by 'an enterprising journalist'. One of the CID chiefs remarked that he could have named him, and the Chief Inspector observed that his name was known to all the heads of the CID.

The letter and postcard themselves bear out this interpretation. They are written without spelling mistakes in an educated hand. They are sent to a news agency, not to a newspaper, which one might have expected a member of the public to target. One is postmarked from the EC postal district, where the newspaper offices stood, not the E postal district where the murders took place. A journalist would have a motive to stir up the story: there had been no murder for two and a half weeks before the first Jack the Ripper missive was penned. Sadly, we have to consign the gory letters to the outer darkness of legends and not clues.

No, there is only one clue that the real Jack the Ripper ever left, and he left it immediately after the Mitre Square murder. We know exactly where he went after killing Katherine Eddowes; we can trace his escape route, and any deductions we make about him must relate to our knowledge of East End topography.

Mitre Square has been rebuilt to an open and airy plan since his day. But he left through the one covered archway passage that remains, leading out to Creechurch Lane. From there he headed east, crossing Duke's Place and Houndsditch. On the night of the double murder, the Aldgate Post Office in Houndsditch was occupied by enterprising burglars who had broken into the buildings. The City Police, though they crowded into the district to investigate the body in Mitre Square, were blandly oblivious to them. In fact they were less competent throughout than the Metropolitan Police in dealing with the Ripper investigation, though their assiduous cultivation of newspapermen saw that they had a better press.

In Goulston Street, huge, gaunt empty tenement buildings still stand, awaiting imminent destruction and redevelopment. Their staircase doorways are bricked up or sealed with heavy padlocked doors; their windows are smashed; bushy weeds sprout from their roofs.

But in 1888 these were the new Wentworth Model Dwellings: up-to-date simple apartments replacing the overcrowded hovels that formerly lined the road. Most of the tenants were Jews, for the buildings are one block away from Petticoat Lane where the Jewish traders sold cheap second-hand clothes on Sunday mornings, and actually front Wentworth Street, the home of the Jewish cheap footwear market.

The Ripper passed these buildings, and dropped his clue in the open doorway nearest to Wentworth Street. There, at 2.50am, PC Alfred Long found half of Katherine Eddowes' apron. So filthy it seemed black rather than white. Made filthier still by the sticky blood still tangible upon it. The murderer had cut off this piece of cloth and used it to wipe his hands, and possibly his knife.

He did not go into the building. Long searched it immediately. Nor does it seem likely, as the City Police speculated, that he was heading for the wicked quarter-mile. He had crossed Goulston Street from east to west instead of proceeding directly along it as he would have done if making for Dorset Street. Topographically it seems most likely that he was making for Wentworth Street with the intention of following it eastward. Two blocks would have brought him to the Princess Alice public house. Two more to the junction of Wentworth Street with old Montague Street. And continuing east, he would have come to the centre of Ripper territory: the same direct road would have carried him almost back to Buck's Row if he followed it to its easternmost extremity.

The only clue the Ripper left strongly endorses the conclusion reached by all sensible commentators, that he was a local East Ender heading for a lair somewhere in the heart of his territory on the Whitechapel/Spitalfields border.

Goulston Street also contained a celebrated non-clue. Chalked on the black brick fascia surrounding the doorway were the mis-spelled words, 'The Juwes are The men That Will not be Blamed for nothing' – or something very like that. Different policemen recorded minor variants of wording, spelling and punctuation.

This notorious graffito was on Metropolitan Police territory. The Met was self-conscious about Jewish associations with the Whitechapel murders after the fiasco of their search for 'Leather Apron'. Moreover, as Chief Inspector Swanson's report to the Home Office stated, the chalk writing was blurred, from which it could be deduced that it was old. PC

Alfred Long who found the apron and the words had no idea whether the words had been there before the apron or not: the walls were covered with graffiti, and he had not paid any attention to them.

True, Detective Constable Daniel Halse of the City force maintained that he had passed earlier, and neither the apron nor the words were there at the time. But Paul Begg has remarked that the City force was so anxious to start its own investigation on the Met's territory that they would have written the words up themselves if it helped! (Not that he believes they did so).

The Met did not believe the graffito was a clue, and they thought it represented a potential danger to Jews in the district. To the fury of City Acting Commissioner Smith, they washed the offending words out without even bothering to photograph them. Major Smith's tirades on the subject have led many unsuspecting historians to claim that these words were written by the Ripper, and sometimes to hang very far-fetched theories from them.

Ripper experts today believe that the Met were perfectly correct to disregard them. They note that the wording, with its cockney double negative, amounts to saying, 'Jews are men who will not take responsibility for anything', and believe it represents an angry response by some Gentile who felt he had come off badly in a deal with a Jew – bought ill-fitting shoes in Wentworth Street, say – and received no satisfaction when, as an unwary buyer, he returned to complain. The Goulston Street clue is the apron, not the chalk writing on the wall.

The Ripper murders were exceedingly well policed. This may seem a daring statement, since book after book has averred that the Met under Sir Charles Warren were a pack of blunderers who allowed the murderer to roam abroad quite unimpeded. It is true that several newspapers made this claim at the time, and true, also, that Warren's resignation was accepted on the morning of the last Ripper murder. But his resignation was the climax of a jurisdictional dispute that had been raging between the Home Office and the Metropolitan

Police Commissioners for fifty years, not a response to the press clamour over the Ripper.

Further, the newspapers that attacked the Met were spearheaded by a radical campaign in the *Star* and the *Pall Mall Gazette* which had been attacking the Met for the previous two years for political reasons. The *Star* was unforgiving about the heavy-handed way in which a mass demonstration of the unemployed had been put down in 1887. And both papers were deeply concerned that the Scotland Yard chiefs had embroiled themselves in a right wing campaign to discredit Parnell and the Irish Nationalist MPs by fraudulently associating them with American-financed terrorism. Both seized on the murders as a means of telling the police, 'Do your job and solve some crimes, and stop playing politics!'

Dispassionate scrutiny since 1987 has suggested that the extra patrols drafted into Whitechapel and Spitalfields were very effective. There was one week between the first murder and the second; three weeks between the second and the night of the double murders; six weeks between the double murders and the last murder: increasing time gaps, which suggest that the extra police on the ground made it harder and harder for the assassin to find his victims unobserved.

It has also been noticed that the police methodology was just what it would be today, except that the lack of sophisticated forensic equipment and laboratories meant that the site-of-crime evidence was not given the thorough going-over it would now, and there were no computers or circular card indexes to store the information brought back by Abberline's detectives.

But those detectives carried out routine house-to-house interviews over the broad area surrounding the murder sites. In Scotland Yard, Assistant Commissioner Anderson and Chief Inspector Swanson sifted through the detectives' noteboooks, sometimes discussing their deductions with the very experienced ex-Assistant Commissioner Monro.

They reached some very firm conclusions: early on, for example, that they were looking for 'Leather Apron' or someone very like him. Later, after the double murders, that they were most likely to find him in an area bounded by Whitechapel Road to the south and Great Garden Street (today's Greatorex Street) to the east.

Some time after the murders were over, they believed that they had got him. But they were unable to charge him; unable to reveal their conclusions to the public; and unnoticed when, in 1910, Anderson did make a half-revelation of the truth. By that time interest in Jack the Ripper was far from intense, and Anderson's memoirs seemed more fascinating for their revelations about police involvement in Irish politics than their veiled references to the Whitechapel murders. (The Irish question was the central political issue when Anderson wrote, and he had much to say about it.)

About half way up Commercial Street, on the left, is a multi-storey car park. Behind the car park in Crispin Street is a yellow-brick convent and night refuge, run by the Sisters of Mercy. It looks down on an unnamed and now private thoroughfare between the car park and the 1930s extension of Spitalfields Market. That thoroughfare is on the line of old Dorset Street. The convent at its western end and the Christ Church burial ground across the road at its eastern end are the only landmarks the Ripper would now recognize.

According to the nuns, Marie Jeanette Kelly took refuge with them in the late 1880s. She was an Irish Catholic girl, and they found her a situation in domestic service with a good family. According to the convent's present solicitor, it was his family, and they have a tradition that the maid they took in from the convent absconded, went on the streets, and perished as the Ripper's last victim.

Marie told her boyfriend a rather more flamboyant tale of her life in London, involving a spell in a West End brothel, and a fully-paid trip to France with a fine gentleman. But the nuns' story seems completely plausible, and there is no doubt that Marie came back to work very close to them.

Miller's Court, Dorset Street was destroyed in the 1930s when the market was extended. It was reached through a dark brick archway. The first door on the right inside the court led into Marie's room, itself partitioned off from the remainder of the house. As the youngest and most attractive of the Ripper's victims, she was also the only one to have a room to herself.

On the evening of 9 November, Marie imbibed a good deal of alcohol. Tradition has it that she did her drinking in the Ten Bells, which still stands beside Christ Church, Spitalfields. The old Victorian blue and white tiles can still be seen on the pub walls, with some early twentieth century panels illustrating eighteenth century Spitalfields let into them. From 1976–88 the pub was renamed the Jack the Ripper, and in that time it accumulated a good deal of Ripperiana, including many of the drawings from the *Illustrated Police Gazette* showing extraordinarily unflattering likenesses of the victims, and rather better representations of the murder sites as they were. The old Jack the Ripper inn sign stands proudly on the bar, and the landlord is familiar with the Ripper experts who often visit the pub.

But in 1988, feminists began to protest that any interest in Jack the Ripper amounted to encouraging men to murder women. They marched through the East End, apparently in the vain hope that an anti-Jack the Ripper march might lead to his being silently forgotten. They disrupted the Whitechapel drama students' end-of-year production of *Jack the Ripper: the Musical*, and they picketed the Jack the Ripper pub demanding that its name be changed and it be prevented from selling commemorative T-shirts and sweatshirts with designs from the *Illustrated Police Gazette*. The landlord and the regulars were unimpressed. But the brewery took fright and had the old name restored. The many foreign visitors to London who have heard of the Jack the Ripper pub and want to visit it now have to ask people in the locality before they can find it.

It may have been in the Ten Bells on the night she was killed that Marie told her friend Lizzie Allbrook she was becoming frightened by the Ripper business, and was contemplating leaving London and going back to Wales where she had previously lived.

Marie was seen going home to Miller's Court, very drunk, around midnight. She was out on the streets again, soliciting, at 2.00am, and probably again at 3.00. Between 3.30 and 4.00am, several residents in Miller's Court heard a cry of 'Murder!' which might have come from Marie's room. They paid no attention. It was a very violent neighbourhood.

The following day Thomas Bowyer was sent from John McCarthy's grocer shop, next to the archway, to collect Marie's heavily overdue rent. When he couldn't open the door, he peeped through the window. The sight he saw on the bed was appalling. Marie had been so totally mutilated and eviscerated that her face was unrecognizable, and, indeed, her carcass could hardly be described as her body.

Hysterical panic swept through London. Sir Charles Warren's resignation was erroneously read as a confession of police incompetence. For the next two years, any East End prostitute found dead with a cut throat was likely to be described as 'another victim of Jack the Ripper'. Yet this was the end. With that final orgy of blood and destruction in a tiny squalid room, lit by a fire of old clothes and a guttering candle, the Ripper apparently shot his bolt and disappeared into the dark and foggy alleys as silently as he had emerged.

So who was he?

Not, I regret to say, Queen Victoria's grandson, the Duke of Clarence. We know where Clarence was on the nights of the murders, and it was never in the vicinity of Whitechapel. On the night of the double murder he was in Scotland, and no means of transport on earth in those days could have carried him down from the grouse moors on Saturday night to return to church on Sunday with a couple of women added to his bag.

Not Sir William Gull, the Queen's physician-in-ordinary. He had suffered a serious stroke the year before, was paralysed down one side, and in no condition to carry out a sequence of murders and mutilations. Nor could any doctor have practised such incompetent butchery as is revealed in Katherine Eddowes' post mortem notes, or the awkward severance of Annie Chapman's bladder.

Not William Gladstone, or Dr Barnardo, or any of the other celebrities whose names are sometimes postulated. They all lived on for years without murdering anyone: a future career incompatible with the obsessive practice of sadistic murder and mutilation.

Nor is there a secret cache of papers in Scotland Yard or the Home Office which will suddenly reveal a great and unsuspected name in 1992. All the official papers in the archives have been open to scholars for years now, and extremely good use has been made of them. Unfortunately, they are bureaucrats' records, not detectives' notebooks. They do not contain the all-important name.

But in 1910 Sir Robert Anderson declared that the Ripper's identity was a positively ascertained fact. He said he was a poor Polish Jew who had been caged in an asylum and then instantly identified when the police confronted him with the only person who had ever had a good sight of the murderer. However, the witness refused to give evidence against the suspect because, as Chief Inspector Swanson added: 'the suspect was also a Jew and also because his evidence would convict the suspect, and witness would be the means of murderer being hanged which he did not wish to be left on his mind.' Not that it would have done any good if the suspect was in an asylum. He could not have been charged.

Two other senior policemen put a name to this suspect. Melville Macnaghten in his set of filed notes, and Donald Swanson in pencilled observations in his copy of Anderson's memoirs both agree that the murderer was called Kozminsky. And the poor Jewish lunatic from Whitechapel, Aaron Kozminsky, has been traced in the records of Mile End Workhouse Infirmary and Colney Hatch Asylum.

Yet a mystery remains. For while there is a preponderance of informed opinion that the Ripper probably *was* a poor Jew from the district, the experts are by no means agreed that he was Aaron Kozminsky. I think he was confused with another very similar patient at Colney Hatch who was the real Ripper. Donald Rumbelow thinks that there is no hard evidence against either of these two men, and Anderson's vague physical description, even alongside his firm assertion, amounts to very little. Richard Whittington-Egan doubts whether Metropolitan policemen of the 1880s would have known a Pole from a Latvian from a Russian, and urges a more intensive study of more asylums to see whether a more probable Ripper has been missed. Paul Begg and Keith Skinner think that being named in two documents and suspected by the City Police puts Kozminsky more firmly in the frame than any other suspect, but they concur that there is much that looks doubtful about him, and really want more evidence.

So there is scope for more work on the Ripper case. But today this work is serious. It will no longer do to pick a name from a hat and airily try to bend the facts about the murders to fit him. Ripper scholars today need to be familiar with the characters of the police investigating the case; with the social and topographical conditions of Whitechapel in the 1880s and with the political stances and biases of the various reporters who created the popular legend.

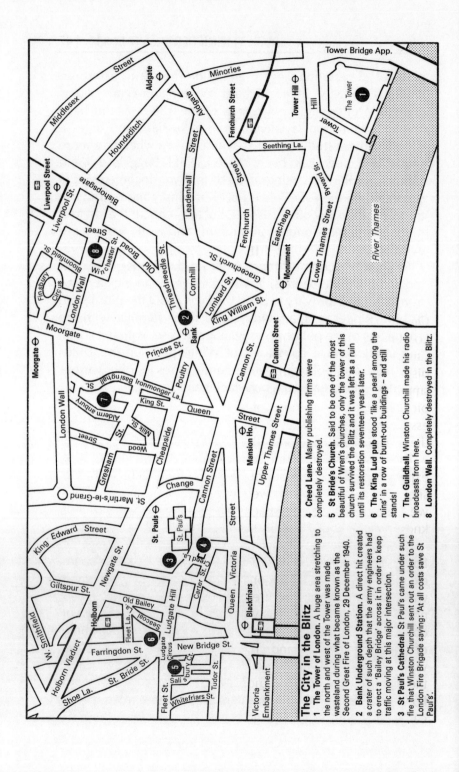

The City in the Blitz

1 The Tower of London. A huge area stretching to the north and west of the Tower was made wasteland during what became known as the Second Great Fire of London, 29 December 1940.

2 Bank Underground Station. A direct hit created a crater of such depth that the army engineers had to erect a 'Bailey Bridge' across it in order to keep traffic moving at this major intersection.

3 St Paul's Cathedral. St Paul's came under such fire that Winston Churchill sent out an order to the London Fire Brigade saying: 'At all costs save St Paul's'.

4 Creed Lane. Many publishing firms were completely destroyed.

5 St Bride's Church. Said to be one of the most beautiful of Wren's churches, only the tower of this church survived the Blitz and it was left as a ruin until its restoration seventeen years later.

6 The King Lud pub stood like a pearl among the ruins' in a row of burnt-out buildings – and still stands!

7 The Guildhall. Winston Churchill made his radio broadcasts from here.

8 London Wall. Completely destroyed in the Blitz.

THE CITY IN THE BLITZ
Roger Tyrrell

One of the most enduring and emotionally striking images of London over the centuries is the photograph of St Paul's Cathedral taken on 29 December 1940. The photograph (on display in the cathedral) shows the building surrounded by smoke made red and orange by fire. More than any other this picture conveys to those of us not there at the time the essence of the Blitz: heroic London, the city that would not die, Britain standing alone, 'Britain can take it'.

Those of us born in London after World War Two experienced the aftermath of the Blitz: the extensive bomb sites, the devastated areas were our playgrounds. As children we revelled in the open spaces (unusual, though we did nót know it at the time, for a city such as London).

At weekends my brother and I would visit the Tower of London, delighting in its gruesome history; but much more exciting were the afternoons spent playing on the great wasteland of rubble and free standing walls that stretched north and west of the Tower where now there is a vast mass of concrete, comprising a car park, windswept plaza, a couple of high-rise blocks and Tower Hill Tube Station. The wasteland was created on one night – 29 December 1940: the night of what became known as the Second Great Fire of London. This chapter tells the story of how those open spaces came into being, and of the great attack on London – the Blitz (so called due to an incorrect understanding of the German term 'Blitzkrieg', meaning 'lightning warfare').

For Britain the Second World War began with the declaration of war on Germany on 3 September 1939. Air raid sirens moaned out over London within minutes of the Prime Minister's radio broadcast to the nation. It was a false alarm. There were to be nine months before the bombs began to fall on England, the period known as 'the Phoney war'.

In May 1940 German troops swept through the Lowlands and into France, which fell within three weeks. The British Expeditionary Force in France retreated to Dunkirk, abandoning most of its heavy equipment, and was evacuated across the Channel. Britain now stood alone against German-occupied Europe.

It was Germany's intention to take Britain out of the war in order to concentrate on attacking the Soviet Union (planned for the following summer). Preferably, political means would be used to achieve this but, if these failed, force would be applied. The German strategy was outlined on 30 June 1940 (three weeks after Dunkirk) by General Jodl, Chief of German Armed Forces Command Staff, in a memorandum entitled 'The Continuation of the War Against England'. This document was produced at Jodl's trial at Nuremberg as Document 1776 PS, and reads as follows:

> If political methods should fail to achieve their objective, England's will to resist must be broken by force.
> a. By attacks on the English homeland.
> b. By an extension of the war peripherally.
> So far as (a) is concerned there are three possibilities:
> 1) Siege.
> This includes attack by land/sea against all incoming and outgoing traffic.
> Attack on the English Air-Arm and on the country's war economy as a whole.
> 2) Terror attacks against English centres of population.
> 3) Invasion with the purpose of occupying England.
> The final victory of Germany over England is now only a

question of time. Offensive enemy operations on a large scale are no longer a possibility.

Jodl's strategy was carried into action with the exception of point 3 – the invasion of England (codenamed 'Operation Sealion'), and it was the Battle of Britain that caused the failure of this scheme.

The *Luftwaffe* assembled two bomber fleets – *Luftflotte II* and *Luftflotte III* – with a combined operational strength of 860 Heinkel 111, Junkers 88A and Dornier medium range bombers based at airfields in Northern France, Belgium and Holland. *Luftflotte II* was commanded by army General Albert Kesselring, based in Brussels. *Luftflotte III* was commanded by Generalfeldmarschall Hugo Sperrle (a veteran of Baron Von Richthofen's World War One 'Flying Circus', as was *Luftwaffe* Commander in Chief Reichsmarschall Hermann Goering) based in Paris.

Operations against England began after Dunkirk with attacks by the *Luftwaffe* on coastal shipping convoys and the dropping of mines in the shipping lanes, thereby pursuing the first of Jodl's strategies. However, impatience with results led to a switch on 19 August 1940 to attacks on radar stations (Dover, Ventnor, etc.) and to attacks on RAF forward fighter stations (those in the immediate area of the Channel, e.g. Tangmere and Manston).

These raids were costly to the *Luftwaffe* as they were operating over British airspace, and so aircrews bailing out of stricken planes became prisoners of war, whereas RAF Fighter Command crews might (and often did) go up again the same day in another plane. Added to this was the fact that British aircraft production was organized on production line methods and was more rapid than German production. The result was that losses for Germany meant an absolute decline in operational strength, whereas Britain's operational strength increased despite heavy losses. Consequently, on 31 August attacks were switched to the RAF Sector Stations covering London. There were seven of these control centres handling fighter operations in London and the South-East; fighters of 11 and 12 Group Fighter Command received battle orders from them. These attacks continued for a week and were proving very damaging; had the *Luftwaffe* sustained its offensive for another week there is little doubt that the ability of the RAF to co-ordinate defence in the battle area would have been destroyed. Strangely and unaccountably, the *Luftwaffe* switched tactics again on 7 September and began the bombing of cities – point 2 of Jodl's strategy. The Blitz had begun.

As early as July 1940, Admiral Raeder, Commander in Chief of the German navy, had urged Hitler to bomb London. Hitler refused because 'the great mass of people cannot be evacuated'. This should not be mistaken for a humanitarian concern; Hilter's aim was to negotiate a peace with Britain and the outrage that would be provoked by bombing London would make this impossible. Conversely, on this side of the Channel Air Marshal Sir Hugh Dowding, Commander in Chief of Fighter Command, was advocating the bombing of German cities as a device to provoke German bombing of English cities. The logic behind this was that it would take pressure off the airfield and the RAF could engage the *Luftwaffe* to advantage over the cities and approaches. Initially neither proponent of civilian bombardment was to have his way.

On 24 August 1940, German bombers attacked the petrol storage depot at Thameshaven (Shellhaven Creek). One or two of the bombers dropped their bombs on central London due to poor navigation and thereby provided the excuse for a retaliatory attack on Germany. The speed with which the RAF reacted clearly shows that they had planned in advance. The very next night (25 August) eighty-one planes of RAF Bomber Command attacked Berlin. Dowding's strategy was about to be realized with a vengeance. On 4 September Hitler announced that he intended to 'wipe out' British cities and rescinded his orders against the bombing of London. Next day Hermann Goering arrived at the Channel coast to take command of the 'Battle of London'.

In the late afternoon of 7 September 300 bombers of

Luftflotten II and *III*, accompanied by 600 fighter escorts, raided the London docks (Woolwich Arsenal, Poplar, Stepney, Bermondsey, West Ham, Victoria and Albert, and the Surrey Commercial docks). The raid came in two waves; the first was attacked by seven squadrons each of 11 and 12 Groups Fighter Command as it turned for home. The second wave was intercepted on the bomb run, but most got through, though bombs fell as far off target as Tottenham (five miles north). Forty-six German planes were shot down for a loss of twenty-eight RAF craft.

On the ground the devastation was appalling. By midnight there were nine fires raging in London that required 100 pumps (fire engines) each, two fires rated 300 pumps and five fires were technically 'out of hand'. A description from *Front Line*, a government publication of 1941, gives a graphic impression of the scene: 'At Woolwich Arsenal men fought the flames among boxes of live ammunition and crates of nitro-glycerine . . . in the docks there were pepper fires, rum fires, paint fires, rubber fires . . . sugar burning in liquid form. . . .' An AFS (Auxiliary Fire Service) man quoted in *Front Line* said, 'Most of us had the wind up to start with especially with no barrage. It was all new, but we were unwilling to show fear however much we might feel it.'

The raids continued by day and night until 18 September, when daylight raiding ceased. On 14 September Hitler postponed his decision on 'Operation Sealion' for three days pending the result of the air battle. The following day the decision was effectively taken for him: 200 bombers and 700 fighters were sent over London, of these 60 were shot down for the loss of 26 RAF fighters – this was the day that is now commemorated as Battle of Britain Day. The bombing continued but on 17 September Hitler cancelled the invasion of Britain.

From 18 September the *Luftwaffe* tried to reduce losses by only mounting night raids, and these continued without break until November, by which time London had been bombed continuously for fifty-two days. Poor weather in late November and early December brought a brief respite, and as

Christmas came and went it seemed that the *Luftwaffe* was on holiday. It was an illusion.

It is time to turn to the scene on the ground in England. Preparations for the defence of Britain against air attack were put in hand after the Munich conference of 1938. Trenches were dug in public parks in London, gas masks issued to the entire population, air raid drills organized. The actual planning of Civil Defence was delegated to the different County authorities, some of which did much, others virtually nothing. A reason for the lack of activity on the part of many County Councils was the anticipated results of civilian bombardment. The Government, heavily influenced by the works of such theorists as the French Air General Douhet, believed that the effects of civilian bombing would be cataclysmic and that preparations to protect civilians would be useless: the only thing to do was to prepare for mass burials, injuries, etc., and contemplate how best order could be maintained in the breakdown of local civilian government that would surely follow city bombing. A clear idea of the popular image of civilian bombing can be drawn from the 1938 Alexander Korda production of H G Wells's *The Shape of Things To Come*. The Home Office, believing that there would be 20,000 civilian dead within the first week of the bombing of London, was largely concerned with the ordering of cardboard coffins, and very few purpose-built bomb shelters were constructed before the Blitz actually began.

However, the County government of London was a different matter. London County Council (LCC) was under the control of the Labour Party led by Herbert Morrison (later Lord Morrison of Lambeth). The LCC was politically at odds with the government, strongly anti-fascist and not at all convinced by Prime Minister Chamberlain's assurances of 'peace in our time'. The LCC consulted with veterans of the British Battalion of the International Brigade, which had fought in the Spanish Civil War. These veterans, led by Tom Wintringham, had experienced the bombing of Madrid by the Italian and German bombers of Mussolini and Hitler, and so had some idea of the likely outcome of such attacks and what could be done to minimize casualties. They advised Morrison that the decisive matter was the reorganization of the Fire Brigade and its expansion to deal with the task ahead.

Morrison heeded this advice. Twenty-eight thousand men and women were recruited to the Auxiliary Fire Brigade and given a brief training course, after which they returned to their regular occupations to await the emergency. The LCC ordered several thousand trailer fire pumps and began the construction of 300 sub-fire stations (the peacetime strength of the LCC Fire Brigade was approximately 4,000 firefighters based on 30 fire stations). The LCC also ordered the manufacture of shelters which could be constructed within the home; steel frames into which three or four people could huddle and so, hopefully, survive the collapse of the building above them. These shelters were known as 'Morrison Shelters' and were later to be superseded by the government issue 'Anderson Shelter' which could be constructed in a back garden. Plans were also commenced to recruit Air Raid Wardens and Heavy Rescue Squads (to dig people out of the ruins); church, school and other halls were marked down for use as local information centres, temporary accommodation for those made homeless by the bombing, etc. Companies were instructed to designate certain employees as fire-watchers and first line fire fighters for their premises. The net result of these and other plans was that London was, if not fully equipped to deal with the onslaught, better prepared than most of the rest of the country.

The Fire Brigade was reorganized throughout the entire London region (which was more extensive than the London County area), with Sir Aylmer Firebrace appointed as Regional Fire Officer commanding sixty-six Fire Brigades from his underground control room at London Fire Brigade headquarters in Lambeth.

When bombing commenced, the casualties, although severe, were on nothing like the scale that had been predicted, yet national and local government feared civilian panic if the full impact were known, as can be seen from this notice posted in West Ham Town Hall:

Official Notice.

The following information has been received from the Ministry of Home Security:

Air Raid Casualties *in the whole of the Metropolitan Police District* between 6.30pm. September 11th and 6.30pm. September 12th were:

Killed 356. Injured and taken to hospital 377.

6.30pm. September 12th and 6.30pm. September 13th: Killed 129. Injured and taken to hospital 185.

6.30pm. September 13th and 6.30pm. September 14th: Killed 265. Injured and taken to hospital 137.

This statement, it is desired, should be posted at the Town Hall and other convenient centres as soon as possible, *but must not be published in the press.*

Mayor and A.R.P. Controller.

West Ham,

Town Hall,

16 September 1940.

In Ministry of Information propaganda films much was made of the shelter provided by underground stations. There are films showing happy Londoners settling down to sleep on tube platforms being serenaded by travelling concert parties. The reality was somewhat different. When the Blitz began the government ordered the closure of the tube stations and troops prevented large crowds at Liverpool Street Station from entering. There were two reasons for this: fear of typhus spread through inevitable lice that would be acquired by masses sleeping in such conditions, and the knowledge that, appearances to the contrary, many stations were not at all deep and would provide little protection. However, popular pressure (and near riots) forced the government to climb down and open the stations, though these only provided accommodation for seven per cent of the London population. The government's fears about the safety of the stations were tragically confirmed when a high explosive bomb hit Balham Underground Station causing the collapse of the tunnel roof, which fractured a water main and drowned 180 people on the platform in a sea of mud.

Ever since the bombing of Berlin in August 1940, Hitler and Goering had been contemplating a raid on London that would obliterate its historic and commercial centre, the City of London – the 'square mile' around St Paul's – and the Bank of England. As yet there were no means to secure the precise concentration of bombs on such an area to ensure its complete destruction, but a means was soon to be available – the X apparatus. The X apparatus or 'Anton Beam' was a system of radio beacon beams which provided cockpit guidance on to targets. The beams were projected from three points on the Channel coast – the primary beam, 'Anton', from Station Anton on the Cherbourg peninsula, secondary beams from Station Cicero at Fécamp, Normandy, and Station Bertha in the Pas de Calais. Bombers would fly along the primary beam (which could be varied in direction) until the secondary beams intersected with it. At the first intersection a signal would be emitted from the receiving apparatus indicating 'ten miles to target'; the second intersection indicated 'over target'. In early November Kampfgeschwader 100, the 'Fire Raisers' were equipped with the new device and acted as pathfinder squadron for the famous raid on Coventry on 12 November 1940 with devastating success.

The success of the Coventry raid led to the planning of an attack on the City of London, which Goering boasted he would 'Coventryize'. Several factors were required for the London raid to have maximum effect: low spring tide in the Thames, low cloud cover, the raid needed to take place on Sunday. Why low tide? The Thames is tidal throughout the London region with two high tides and two low tides a day; the rise and fall varies between fifteen to twenty-six feet at London Bridge, and once a month the low tide is such that the river is reduced to a stream about ten feet wide at London Bridge. The *Luftwaffe* knew that their high explosive bombs would soon fracture the City water mains and leave only the river as a fall-back for the Fire Brigade. Low cloud at about 5,000 feet was required as a shield against anti-aircraft fire since KG 100 would lead the raid at 6,000 feet, thereby ensuring maximum accuracy of bomb placement. Sunday was the day on which the City would be virtually deserted, its office workers at home in the suburbs, and consequently no key-holders in the office buildings. This would leave the Fire Brigade forced to break into buildings set alight by incendiary bombs which would have generated intense fire by the time this had been achieved. All these factors came together on Sunday 29 December 1940.

Early on the Sunday morning, Hugo Sperrle (General Commanding *Luftflotte III*) received a call direct from Führer HQ Berlin ordering him to organize a raid on the City of London that night. Sperrle called a planning conference in his headquarters at the Hotel Luxembourg with General Kesselring (commanding *Luftflotte II*) attending. The plan evolved was that some 300 bombers of both *Luftflotten* would attack with incendiary bombs and high explosives in a series of waves beginning at 6.05pm (British time) that night. There would be two sorties per plane with the aircraft rearming, refuelling and returning to the attack.

The bomber squadrons involved would be led by KG 100 based at Vannes in Brittany. KG 100 was largely staffed by pre-war aircrews, infinitely more experienced than the crews of other squadrons, where the average age was nineteen. The squadron commander was Hauptmann Friedrich Aschenbrenner, who had led the raid against Coventry and also bombed Rotterdam and Warsaw. Aschenbrenner had earlier flown with the Condor Legion in Spain and may well have bombed Guernica too. KG 100 was equipped with twenty special Heinkel 111 H2s, fitted with the X apparatus, and of higher performance than the standard He 111.

KG 100 would strike first, lighting up the target through the clouds as a beacon to the later squadrons. It would be followed wave on wave by the other squadrons: KG 27 (2 wings of 40 planes), KG 54 (2 wings of 40 planes), KG 51 (1 wing of 20 planes), and LG 1 (Lehrgeschwader – Demonstration Bomb Group) with 3 wings totalling 60 planes. These squadrons, based at stations in Brittany, Normandy, Orléans and Orly near Paris, would be backed by several squadrons from *Luftflotte II* based in the Lowlands, bringing the total strength to 300 bombers. An escort of 600–700 fighters would be provided.

The bombers would be armed with high explosive and/or incendiary bombs. Each Heinkel or Ju 88 with a bomb capacity of 4,400 lbs, could carry 8 550lb high explosive bombs (HEs) or 8 canisters of 36 incendiary bombs (IBs). The incendiary bomb canisters were known as 'Molotov Breadbaskets' and would open at a pre-set altitude, showering the bombs over the target area. Each IB was one foot long and about three inches in diameter at the base, which tapered conically to a point. Each contained one kilo of magnesium that would generate a heat of 4,000°F in one minute and burn for ten. IBs were easily extinguished if caught early on by shovelling sand on them or smothering them with a fire blanket. The most dangerous (in fact almost suicidal) thing to do was to douse them with water. Many IBs would fall harmlessly to burn spectacularly in the street, but others would punch their way through rooftops to become lodged in the rafters and so ignite the building; the soft lead roofs of the City's Wren churches were particularly vulnerable to these devices. Once HEs had blown gaping holes in buildings they would be open to the showers of IBs falling into them. Later in the Blitz, tackling IBs was made more dangerous by the inclusion of an explosive charge.

Dusk fell over southern England at 5.30 on the evening of the 29th. The Black-out (the wartime ban on lights showing from buildings) began at 5.26pm. By this time Hauptmann Aschenbrenner was already on his way.

Aschenbrenner's squadron had received orders for the attack on 'LOGE' (codename for London) at 12.30pm and took off from Vannes at 4.30pm. KG 100 circled over the Gulf of St Malo and Aschenbrenner reported at 5.20pm that he had locked into Anton Beam over Cherbourg with an estimated forty-eight minutes to target. The bombers headed for the English coast, crossing it near Bognor Regis at 5.47pm. On the English side of the Channel, KG 100 was picked up at 5.15pm by Ventnor radar station, Isle of Wight, as the

Heinkels assembled in battle formation. RAF Fighter Command HQ at Stanmore, Middlesex, was informed and in turn alerted 11 Group, Fighter Command at sector control Uxbridge. Uxbridge in turn alerted sector airfields at Tangmere (Kent), Kenley (Surrey) and Gravesend (Kent) to stand by. As Aschenbrenner crossed the coast, 219 Squadron, Tangmere, scrambled its Beaufighter night fighters (equipped with A1 MK IV cockpit radar). These, however, failed to make contact with the raiders. At 5.58pm Aschenbrenner's Heinkel passed over Mitcham, Surrey, and the first buzzer, 'ten miles to target', sounded in his cockpit.

London was as yet unaware of the great airfleet heading towards it. At 5.26pm the bells of St Bride's church, Fleet Street (most beautiful of Wren's City churches) sounded out at the end of service. It was the last time the bells would be heard for seventeen years. At 5.58pm, when the flight line of the incoming aircraft made it clear they were heading straight for London, Air Marshal 'Sholto' Douglas (Fighter Command Operations Room, Stanmore) called Home Office Fire Control Room (Commander Firebrace) with the news that 'a large formation' was on its way to London and, seven minutes later, the sirens began to moan out along the South London approaches.

As the sirens sounded to the south, George Garwood, in charge of the permanent staff of St Paul's Cathedral Fire Watch, received a phone call from the roof informing him of the alert. He made ready to go upstairs, but first received a second call telling him of IBs falling across the river in Southwark. By the time Mr Garwood had climbed to the rooftop, IBs were falling all round in heavy showers and bouncing off the dome of the cathedral.

With cloud at 4,500 feet all over southern England and London itself, Aschenbrenner could not see his target and was flying blind. At 6.08pm the second buzzer in his cockpit sounded out and Aschenbrenner's bombardier released his deadly cargo. The IBs straddled Guy's Hospital, Southwark, London Bridge Railway Station and the River Thames. They were a thousand yards short of the target – the Bank of

England – though in the circumstances they had achieved remarkable accuracy. Bombs away, Aschenbrenner ascended a few thousand feet to circle and observe the rest of his squadron's performance. The following bombers achieved even greater accuracy, hitting areas around St Paul's, Moorgate just north of the Bank, and the area around the Tower of London.

On the ground at Guy's Hospital, surgeons were at work in a temporary operating theatre. The IBs pierced the roof of the theatre and the surgeons ordered nurses to douse them with sand while continuing the operation. Outside the hospital, in nearby Tooley Street, Mrs Florence Welsh was closing down her mobile tea canteen for the night. Suddenly the whole street was lit by the bright flare of burning incendiaries. Mrs Welsh resignedly filled up her water boiler to make tea and 'stood by to receive firemen'. She would have a long night ahead of her.

Over at Guildhall – the City Hall of the City of London – the firewatch commanded by Mr F A George was desperately trying to protect the early fifteenth century building, one of the few survivors of the Great Fire of 1666. At 6.25pm Mr George ordered all sand buckets refilled and it was reported to him that all IBs had been extinguished. He could not know it, but this was only for the moment.

By now whole areas of Southwark, Islington and the City itself were in the grip of fires burning out of control. At 6.30pm Aschenbrenner turned for home, sending a radio message to Sperrle: 'Target bombed, fierce fires raging, more bombers approaching'.

At 6.20pm Major Shulz-Hein, commanding I Wing KG 51, was approaching London, leading the second squadron on this fire-raising night. Shulz-Hein thought the whole raid was idiotic, conducted as it was in a blanket of low cloud. His semi-pubescent air-crews wanted to know how they were to find the target. Shulz-Hein didn't know. Even more importantly, how were they to find their way back home? For this Shulz-Hein had an answer – hadn't they heard of the compass and dead-reckoning? Nevertheless, Major Shulz-

Hein was a worried man as he flew blind towards a target he thought he would never find. Then, as he flew over Dorking, Shulz-Hein saw a 'rose glow through the cloud' – the fires of KG 100 marking the way to the City of London.

There was no perceptible pause in the bombing as far as people on the ground were concerned, but at 6.30pm Aschenbrenner left the scene of the crime and Major Shulz-Hein moved in. KG 51 managed a concentration of HE mixed with IBs on the Paternoster Row and Square area, immediately north of St Paul's.

Before the war Paternoster Row had been the centre of the publishing trade in England. Indeed, back in the Great Fire of London in 1666, when Paternoster Row was burned down for the first time, 500,000 books went up in smoke. On this evening in December fifteen million volumes were to make a similar exit. The offices and stores of twenty-seven publishing firms were destroyed. The employees of the publishing firms were members of St Paul's fire watch, running on ropes around the cathedral dome hacking out IBs as their own workplaces burned down across the street. After this night, publishing moved out, mainly to the Bloomsbury area around the British Museum, and has never returned. By 6.30pm, fire-watchers on St Paul's were reporting 'fires out of control' in the buildings without fire-watchers in the area.

By 6.30pm New Change opposite St Paul's was a continuous blaze. Carter Lane to the south of the cathedral was an inferno, and on the cathedral itself the fire-watchers were now using wet sacks to put out flying sparks landing from other conflagrations.

At 6.39pm St Paul's Fire Watch phoned Cannon Street Fire Station to report that the dome was on fire. This was true but turned out to be no real threat. An IB had punched into the lead of the dome and was blazing away. The blaze lit up the whole dome and shone through the windows at the base of the drum. The IB was only partially embedded in the lead and its own heat melted the lead, causing it to fall to the floor of the Stone Gallery where it burned on harmlessly. It was this bomb that gave rise to Ed Morrows' CBS broadcast to America that night.

Morrow was watching the bombing from the roof of the Press Association building in Fleet Street, and, as was his habit, was holding his microphone aloft to catch the sound of the bombs as they fell around him, conveying a vivid impression to his listeners back home in the States.

Morrow said, 'And the church that meant most to Londoners is now gone. St Paul's Cathedral, built by Sir Christopher Wren, her great dome towering over the capital of the Empire, is burning to the ground as I talk to you'. Morrow was understandably wrong. At the same time Prime Minister Winston Churchill had sent out an order to the London Fire Brigade: 'At all costs save St Paul's'. Divisional Officer Cyril Demarne responded, 'He didn't need to tell us that'.

By 6.45pm St Bride's, where only an hour earlier a service to welcome the New Year had been celebrated, was a blazing inferno. There was no fire-watch stationed in the church and it simply burned. But St Bride's is the 'Newspapermen's church' and so night porters at the nearby Reuters, Press Association, and Press Club broke into the church and rescued what they could. They had just carried out a brass lectern that had been similarly saved from the Great Fire of 1666, when the roof collapsed, leaving the church a ruin until its restoration by Lord Beaverbrook some seventeen years later.

By this time other bombers were homing in on target, although some were dropping their bombs wildly off the mark. Bombs were now falling on Croydon (twelve miles to the south) and Hampstead (five miles to the north). Yet most crews were still bombing with great accuracy.

It was now 6.53pm, fifty-eight minutes after the first bombs had fallen, but the Fire Brigade crews remained in their stations awaiting orders. There were two simple reasons for this: to send fire pumps out as the bombs were falling would be to sacrifice men and equipment needlessly; secondly, Fire Control was waiting to build up a picture of the areas most heavily affected by the bombs so that they could develop a strategy for fighting the fires in a manner which they might hope to win. At precisely 6.53pm, Commander Firebrace alerted every fire station in the 100 square mile LCC area. The first 'Bells Down' sounded at Ambler Road AFS (Auxiliary Fire Service) Station in Finsbury just north of the City. AFS Firemen James Mayers and his crew were sent to Guildhall – where they found they were not wanted! They were then sent to Aldersgate Street Fire Station which was 'well alight' – it was the crew's first fire!

Yet not every fireman waited for the bells to 'go down'. Station Officer Laurence Odling at Whitefriars Fire Station could not, as a regular fireman, stand and watch the bombs fall and the fires rise. He scrambled his crews in the general direction of Fleet Street. Odling's directions were to look for fires and put them out. His own pump worked along Fleet Street, stopping first at St Clement Danes church to extinguish a blaze, and carried on down fighting fires wherever they found them.

Sudden promotions were now taking place: Sub-Officer Frank Lawrence at Lambeth Fire Brigade HQ was ordered to take two telephonists to Guildhall and take command there in what was the City of London Fire Control Centre.

By 7.00pm the General Post Office (postal headquarters) in King Edward Street was abandoned, all telegraph cables for international communications being severed (although these would be restored by 4.00pm the following afternoon). Fires were now burning in several areas as continuous blazes; for example, in an area from Fleet Street north into Barbican (¾ mile by ¼ mile) and an area by the Tower radiating out from the Minories. Across the river, a mile-long stretch of riverside warehouses was ablaze from Waterloo to Tower Bridge. George Garwood on St Paul's watched the Central Telephone Exchange burn to the ground 'without a bucket of water to put on it'. At Whitecross Street Fire Station fire-eroded buildings collapsed, blocking all exits. The firemen managed to get out but had to abandon twelve pumps which melted in the blaze. About this time the steeple of St Lawrence-in-the-Jewry-next-Guildhall was struck by an IB. Guildhall Fire Watch phoned Cannon Street Fire Station but they were fully occupied, the church was locked and in any case Guildhall could not spare anyone to climb the steeple – they mournfully watched it burn on through the night.

It was at this time (7.00pm) that Commander Firebrace decided to take a tour of the fireground with his deputy Mr A P L Sullivan. In his memoirs Firebrace tells us that London Bridge Railway Station was 'well alight' and that the situation in Queen Victoria Street was 'ugly'. Firebrace believed the German claim that they had dropped 100,000 IBs that night – he had every reason to: in fact the true figure was around 24,000.

Water was now in short supply – three of the 36 inch mains in the City and twelve other large mains were fractured. The demand on the remaining supplies reduced pressure to a trickle. The tide was now out and Divisional Officer Cyril Demarne of West Ham Fire Brigade saw firefloat crews wading through the mud of the Thames to place hoses in the diminutive stream left by London Bridge. Demarne, a former merchant sailor, knew that New Fresh Wharf on the north bank by London Bridge had a dredged channel to enable ships to berth at all times of tide and this constituted a reserve pool of water. He ordered hoses lowered into the water from the bridge, but this supply could not last for long.

By 8.00pm there were 300 fire pumps operating in the City. Redcross Street Fire Station in the Barbican was receiving calls at the rate of one every thirteen seconds. And still the bombs were falling. At Fire Brigade Northern Division HQ, Divisional Officer Francis Peel had worked out an impromptu method of gauging the intensity and concentration of the fires: he placed a pin on the map for every reported fire and built up a series of clusters that showed the areas most in need.

As the evening continued, separate fires became area conflagrations. In the narrow thoroughfares of the City flames arced across the street to join hands. Firemen had to be tied to strongpoints to prevent the winds caused by the intake of air to the fires sweeping them away. A fireman collapsed with an IB embedded in his back. Others were blinded by smoke or flying sparks. Strange events were occurring; a crew fighting a massive blaze suddenly found it extinguished by the blast from a high explosive bomb landing nearby.

In King William Street, Cyril Demarne and his fellow officers from West Ham were laying hoses from the Thames north past the Bank to Moorgate, with relay pumps every regulation 700 feet. By morning the fire hoses would be three feet deep along this route. Demarne was also learning lessons in sexual politics: he had set up a control point, a desk in the open on King William Street, and was giving directions to a queue of firemen. A firewoman stepped forward and Demarne told her he was too busy to deal with her trivia at present. She went to the back of the queue. When she made it to the front again Demarne dismissively asked her her problem; she replied that she had a 500 gallon petrol tanker parked across the road (to refuel fire pumps) and would like to know where to deliver it! In his memoirs Demarne tells us that it was at this point he realized the situation of the firewomen: not allowed to take the glory of fighting the fires, but able to drive through an inferno in a mobile bomb!

The bombers continued, wave on wave, until 11.40pm when the last incendiary bomb was reported at No 5 Creed Lane. A few minutes later at 11.50pm the all-clear sounded out to the dismay and disbelief of the firefighters on the ground. They knew from previous raids that a second wave would surely follow, dropping HEs to stoke up the fires and cause further fatalities among the firemen. This was indeed General Sperrle's plan. But now the weather had further deteriorated over northern France and some of the returning bombers crash-landed on their airfields. Hauptmann Aschenbrenner knew there would be no second sortie and went to bed. Major Shulz-Hein was outraged to receive orders for a second strike and tried to have them rescinded. He pointed out that even in good weather his crews would be dog-tired by now and it would be suicidal to attempt take-offs and landings in these conditions. He was told to re-arm. Major Shulz-Hein did not expect to survive the night. However, at 12.30 orders came through to stand down: the second wave was cancelled.

Had the second strike come the firemen were in no doubt that it would have created a firestorm – the phenomenon that destroyed Hamburg and Dresden – and that the City would have ceased to exist. As it was, by midnight fires along Moorgate were generating air temperatures of 1,000°C, the condition necessary for firestorm, but fortunately the areas affected were contained in extent and did not create sufficient indraughts of air.

By 11.00pm Guildhall had been abandoned, its roof collapsing in flames. Next morning the City Fire Watch would raise the Union Jack over its blackened walls; Winston Churchill would later make defiant radio broadcasts from its shell, and in 1945 General Eisenhower would broadcast the news of the German surrender from the ancient hall. But this was all in the future. For now, the firefight continued on the ground.

Firebrace was continuing his tour of the fires. He described the situation in the Barbican:

> The high wind which accompanies conflagrations is now stronger than ever, and the air is filled with a fierce driving rain of red-hot sparks and burning brands. The clouds overhead are a rose-pink from the reflected glow of the fires, and fortunately it is light enough to pick our way eastward down Fore Street. Here fires are blazing on both sides of the road; burnt-out and abandoned fire appliances lie smouldering in the roadway, their rubber tyres completely melted. The rubble from the collapsed buildings lying three and four feet deep, makes progress difficult in the extreme. Scrambling and jumping, we use the bigger bits of fallen masonry as stepping stones, and eventually reach the outskirts of the stricken area.

Firebrace noted that the Barbican area had long been known to firemen as the 'Danger Zone'. Its streets were very narrow and its old-fashioned buildings complied with few fire regulations. There were many warehouses, workshops and offices that represented a 'torch waiting for a flame'.

By midnight there were six area conflagrations needing

more than one hundred pumps each, twenty-eight requiring over thirty pumps, fifty at the twenty-pump mark, one hundred needing ten and 1,286 fires which 'had to make do with one pump apiece'. Two thousand fire pumps of the London Regional Brigades were at work, backed by 300 more from the surrounding regions. Before the war there were 1,850 fire pumps in the whole of Great Britain.

By 2.30am the firemen were tired and hungry. Publicans in the City were opening their pubs and giving them free beer. Fireman Rosefield and his mates were drinking outside a pub in 'an alleyway near St Bride's' (either the Old Bell or the Punch Tavern). At the same time Sub-Officer Wilmott and his crew were approached by an elderly lady with a carrier bag who asked 'Would the firemen like a sandwich?' Wilmott and his men agreed instantly and took their sandwiches to a nearby pub where he remembers that if they had accepted all the free pints offered they would have got 'well and truly plastered'. This generosity on the part of the publicans does not seem to have gone unrewarded: at 8.30 next morning Mr T R Tower crossed the river into the City at Blackfriars Bridge and was struck by the undamaged pubs on New Bridge Street – the Blackfriar, the Albion and the King Lud standing 'like pearls among the ruins' in the row of burnt-out buildings!

The firefighting continued throughout the night and Firebrace reports that by 8am the 'situation was in hand'. Many buildings continued to burn through the day but the Fire Service prided itself on extinguishing flames before the next nightfall so that they would not provide a beacon for the night raiders. This was achieved but 'damping down' operations continued for another three days.

Cyril Demarne recalls seeing the office workers picking their way over the fire hoses and rubble on their way to workplaces that might or might not still exist. The firemen covered in filth, their eyes reddened by smoke, were disconsolately sitting in the streets pouring water out of their boots. Demarne recalls with gratitude that many workers dumbstruck by the devastation silently took their sandwiches out of their briefcases and gave them to the firemen. They went on their way to find that their offices no longer existed or that the shells were awash with water. Most buildings were without electricity and heating, all telephone lines were out: it took days to clear up the mess.

Workers in the City and those people with a view of it were astounded to see St Paul's rising above the smoking ruins. The cathedral had been hit by hundreds of IBs but the fire-watchers had extinguished every one of them. St Paul's was also hit by three high explosive bombs during the Blitz. One, a 500lb HE, came through the roof of the north transept and exploded in the crypt against the foundations of the dome. A survey showed that the foundations had not moved even by a fraction of an inch. Another 500lb HE exploded between the roof and the false ceiling over the high altar, destroying the interior east end of the church. This is now occupied by the American Memorial Chapel, in memory of all those US servicemen who lost their lives operating out of Britain in World War Two. Finally, a 1,000lb HE hit the pavement in front of the western portico of the church. It failed to explode but was burrowing its way down towards the foundations of the main entrance under its own weight. A team of Canadian military engineers chased it down and prevented its detonation. It was taken by truck to Hackney Marshes in East London where the detonation caused a 100 foot crater. Had this bomb exploded at St Paul's it would have taken about half the cathedral with it.

People far from the City now became aware of the momentous events. Mrs G White, living at her parents' house in Upminster, Essex, opened her front door to get the milk and found the porch covered in a thick layer of burnt papers. On examination they proved to be accounts from ledger books in the City of London. The column of smoke rising from the City could be seen in Oxford, fifty miles away.

Now was the time to count the cost and survey the damage done. The BBC laconically announced that 'last night enemy bombers attacked towns in Southern England, causing some casualties'. The Luftwaffe was unaware of the extent of the destruction and General Sperrle regarded the raid as a failure since the second wave did not strike. Aerial reconnaissance was impossible as the low cloud still hung over the target city. However, the official *Luftwaffe* report states, 'Rarely if ever were fires of such number and size perceived during a single attack against the capital.'

Sixteen firemen had been killed and 250 detained in hospital, largely with temporary blindness, but many with severe burns and smoke-damaged lungs. One hundred and sixty-three civilians had been killed (largely living in the residential areas immediately outside the City), and 509 had been seriously injured. St Bartholomew's Hospital in the City had received 123 casualties in the course of the night.

Seven areas had been completely burned out. Looking at a map of the city, the areas can be traced along the streets. The first ran along Beech Street and Chiswell Street, turning north to take in the Artillery Ground with a northern limit at Bunhill Fields, south along Moorgate to Gresham Street, turning south again at Milk Street down to Cheapside, then south at Bread Street to Queen Victoria Street running along as far as Bracken House, next turning south to the riverside, along the river to Blackfriars, along both sides of New Bridge Street, turning west at Tudor Street, north again to cross Fleet Street running back east to the railway line at Seacoal Lane, north into Old Bailey along Newgate Street, crossing over to Christchurch Newgate Street and the Post Office's King Edward Building, then turning onto Aldersgate Street running north to complete the area at Beech Street. This was the largest area of devastation.

Another area was bounded by Chancery Lane on the west, Holborn on the north, Shoe Lane on the east and Fleet Street on the south. The third area ran along Queen Street on the west, Cannon Street on the north, London Bridge on the east and the river on the south. The fourth area covered Leadenhall Street at the north, bounded by the Tower and Fenchurch Street to the east and ran south from Leadenhall Street down to Lower Thames Street. Area five was from Houndsditch on the south to Middlesex Street on the north, with its eastern boundary reaching nearly to Bishopsgate. The sixth area was the zone mentioned at the beginning of this chapter: centring on the Minories, it encompassed the stretch from Aldgate Bus Station down to the river south and west of the Tower. The seventh area was across the river in Southwark. The riverfront from Tower Bridge to London Bridge consisted entirely of burned-out warehouses, with the destruction stretching back through London Bridge Railway Station and along Borough High Street as far as St Thomas's Street.

All mainline railway termini were out of action with the exception of Liverpool Street Station. Hundreds of banks, offices and warehouses were gutted wrecks. But it was the destruction of the Wren churches which gripped the minds of the press and public.

The City was never an area distinguished for the beauty of its buildings. The old offices of the City had a certain aggregate charm and character. The Livery Halls of the City's Guilds were opulent structures, some with splendid interior woodwork and fine collections of gold and silverware, but they tended to express corporate wealth and pomp rather than good taste. It was Sir Christopher Wren's churches which represented what was most glorious and beautiful in this commercial capital.

Wren, the architect to the King in the years after the Great Fire of 1666, had built fifty churches in the 'Square Mile' apart from St Paul's Cathedral. This may sound a little excessive, but eighty-nine churches had been destroyed by the fire, so Wren had in fact rationalized with his fifty new buildings. Wren was a Classical architect, moving over to Baroque towards the end of his long career. Each church had a distinct appearance; each tower or steeple some mark of individuality to distinguish it from the surrounding forest of spires; the interiors, richly decorated with plaster were tranquil refuges for contemplation away from the noise and bustle of the City.

Time, and more particularly the Victorians, had dealt harshly with these churches. Between 1870 and 1890 nearly twenty had been demolished to make way for banks. A stroll round the environs of the Bank of England reveals a mournful succession of blue plaques commemorating these victims of Victorian arrogance. Now ten more Wren churches stood in ruins.

The principal parish church of the City was a wreck – St Mary le Bow on Cheapside had once been the church of the Archbishop of Canterbury when resident in London. With its great bell, it stood on the main market street (in Old English a 'cheap' is a market). The bell rang out in former centuries to signal the curfew; to be born within the sound of it was to be a 'cockney' or a Londoner. When the church was bombed the bell fell out of the tower and melted. In a sense, there would be no more true-born Londoners until 1956, when the bell was recast.

Reference has already been made to the destruction of St Bride's on Fleet Street. The interior of the church was somewhat marred by the Victorian pews, but it was its steeple that attracted affection. St Bride's steeple is a series of concentric drums reducing as they ascend, and it gave rise to the design of the tiered wedding cake, the church itself being known as the 'wedding cake church'. St Lawrence-in-the-Jewry-next-Guildhall, the church of the government of the City, had burned before the eyes of the Guildhall fire-watchers, its steeple crashing down in flames into the body of the church.

St Alban's, Wood Street, was likewise a shell and later the authorities would seize the opportunity to demolish the remains of the body, leaving only the tower, since the church stood in the middle of a narrow street. The church of Christchurch, Newgate Street, stood next to the postal headquarters, and as it blazed two postmen rushed into the furnace to rescue what they could. They seized the carved font cover made by Grinling Gibbons, Wren's master woodcarver, and this now resides in the church of the Holy Sepulchre-without-Newgate. Here, too, there would be no restoration as the City Corporation wished to broaden the curve at the corner of Newgate Street. The remains of the church are now a garden dominated by the old tower.

St Olave's church on Ironmonger Lane would have its body replaced by a new one, but finally became an estate agent's office. St Nicholas Cole Abbey on Queen Victoria Street, the church of the Hudson Bay Company, with a weather vane in the shape of the *Nonsuch* – the company's first ship – would be restored to use. The church of St Andrew by the Wardrobe on Queen Victoria Street had been badly abused by Victorian beautifiers and would now suffer the further indignity of having an office built in its interior to house the Society for Ancient Monuments. The little brick church of St Anne and St Agnes, the cheapest of Wren's churches with only a wooden turret instead of a tower, would be restored to become a Lutheran Church with services in Latvian, Lithuanian and Estonian.

Tucked away behind the cathedral was the minuscule church of St Augustine, the church of St Paul's Choir School. Here only the tower was left standing. A committee of architects called the Architects Co-partnership would conspire to erect a bizarre replacement built of concrete and lead in the modernist style. It is difficult to imagine anything more incongruous with the Wren tower and the great cathedral next to it.

Strangest of all was the fate reserved for the church of St Mary Aldermanbury, on Love Lane. In 1966 the remains of the church were shipped to Fulton, Missouri, USA, where the restored church now stands as a memorial to Winston Churchill's 'Iron Curtain' speech made at Westminster College, Fulton, in 1946.

The bombing of London and other cities in Britain continued after the night of the 'Second Great Fire'. On the 11 January 1941 a direct hit on Bank Underground Station blasted a great crater in the middle of the road, under which lay the station ticket office. Bodies were thrown up from the station and scattered all around. The crater was of such depth that army engineers had to erect a bailey bridge across it for traffic at this major intersection.

During mid-January to mid-March there were a number of minor raids known as 'nuisance raids'. On 8 March there was a heavy raid of 125 bombers, then from March through to mid-April an average of one raid per week, the heaviest of these being on 19 March, when there were 479 bombing sorties dropping 400 tons of high explosive. On 16 and 19 April there were two heavy raids. These were remembered by Londoners as 'The Wednesday' and 'The Saturday'. 'The Wednesday' saw the destruction of Chelsea Old Church, the church of Sir Thomas More. On 'The Saturday' St Paul's was hit again.

The worst raid of the entire Blitz came on 10 May 1941 when bombs fell for six and a half hours. Westminster Abbey, the British Museum and the Tower of London were hit (the bomb in the Tower causing a total casualty list of one raven). Overall, the raid killed 1,436 civilians and injured 1,800 more.

Londoners could not know it, but the raid of 10 May was the last of the period we call the Blitz. The campaign had severely depleted the operational strength of the *Luftwaffe* bomber fleets. The two *Luftflottes* had a combined strength of 860 on 1 September 1940; this was down to 820 on 1 October; by 1 December it had declined to 700. The average number of bombers over target also declined from 197 in September 1940 to 134 in October, and was down to 120 by January 1941.

Now the *Luftwaffe* had other tasks ahead of it, and on 11 May 1941 *Luftflotte II* flew to Poznan in Poland to begin preparations for the invasion of the Soviet Union on 22 June. For Hauptmann Aschenbrenner this would be his last campaign: he would die bombing Russia in 1943. *Luftflotte III* was detached to bomb North Africa, with a skeletal force left in northern Europe.

By 11 May 1941 more than 20,000 Londoners had died in the bombing and more would yet follow. Between 7 September 1940 and 10 May 1941 one in six Londoners were made homeless and 1,500,000 houses damaged to one degree or another. Throughout Britain in this period 200,000 houses were totally destroyed and 3,700,000 damaged.

After the invasion of the Soviet Union the bombers returned

with the 'Little Blitz' of late 1941/1942. Though damaging and harrowing for those affected, it was by no means the fearful onslaught of the Blitz proper. The over-extended military commitment of Germany to war on several fronts meant that never again was the *Luftwaffe* able to mount a similar bombing campaign against mainland Britain. They had not, however, abandoned plans for bombing altogether. In 1942 development work was begun on a new weapon – the flying bomb.

An aerial reconnaissance officer, Wing-Commander Kendall, had detected strange ramps being constructed at Peenemünde on the Baltic coast in late 1942. At the time it was not known what these might be. Professor Lindemann, the government's Chief Scientific Adviser dismissed suggestions that they might be rocket launching sites. But by October 1943 the military intelligence services, using the 'Ultra machine' (a decoding device that enabled Britain to read all coded German communications throughout the war), had made intercepts of radio broadcasts of the German 14th Company of Experimental Signal Engineers. This company had installed radios in the experimental V1 rockets being tested at Peenemünde and, by late autumn, London was being informed of the performance of each bomb as soon as, if not sooner than, Berlin. It was now known that the air speed of the bomb was 400 mph, and that its accuracy was increasing. Then on 3 November 1943 six sites with ramps similar to those at Peenemünde were detected in northern France (these were dubbed 'ski sites'), and it was observed that the ramps all pointed in the direction of London. By 22 November ninety-five 'ski sites' had been identified and were heavily bombed by the RAF and USAAF. However, the sites were being constructed at a more rapid pace than they could be destroyed.

On 16 May 1944, Feldmarschall Keitel announced, 'the bombardment will open like a thunderclap in the night'. It was Keitel's intention that the first rockets would be launched against London before dawn on 20 April with an initial launch of 300, to be followed at noon by another 100, and

200 more as night fell. Keitel, though, was overruled by Hitler, who told Goebbels, 'The revenge bombardment is going to be synchronized with their invasion.' This did not quite come to pass because of technical problems with the bomb and its launching sites. The Allies invaded France on 6 June 1944, but it was not until 13 June that the first V1s were launched against England.

Far from Keitel's hundreds, only ten V1s were launched that day, and of these five crashed in the sea, one completely vanished and four went on to fall on England. The first rocket bomb landed in a field at Swanscombe near Gravesend in Kent at 4.13am. It severely damaged a nearby house but there were no casualties. Two other bombs exploded at Cuckfield, Sussex, and at Platt, near Sevenoaks, Kent, without any casualties. However, the fourth bomb fell on London. This exploded on a railway bridge at Grove Road, Bow, East London. The bridge did not collapse but the railway line below was torn up – this was the main Chelmsford to Liverpool Street line. Two nearby houses were completely destroyed and several others damaged; six people were killed, ten were seriously injured, twenty-four were detained in hospital, and two hundred rendered homeless. The 'doodlebugs' had arrived.

The V1 flying bomb was twenty-five feet long and two feet in diameter. Powered by an impulse jet engine it carried a warhead of 1,870lbs of Amatol (TNT and ammonium nitrate). The entire bomb weighed nearly two tons and had a range of about 150 miles, it could reach speeds of up to 400 mph, and cruised at between 1,000 and 6,000 feet. The engine noise resembled a screaming motor bike or 'a Model T Ford struggling up a hill'. The rocket could be adjusted to cut out and dive at a pre-set distance, and the majority were pre-set to hit the Bank of England. However, variations in wind-speed, fuel and other factors caused most of the bombs to fall elsewhere (in fact none ever hit the Bank).

In all 5,823 V1s landed on mainland Britain. Many others were shot down or 'toppled' (knocked off course by fighters flying alongside and flipping them with their wing tips) over the Channel; still more were exploded by anti-aircraft batteries on the coast. Of the total which made it, 41 per cent – 2,242 – landed in the London area, with Kent (1,444) and Sussex (880) next in the league. 6,184 civilians and 2,917 servicemen were killed, 23,000 houses were destroyed.

The advance of the Allies from the Normandy beaches through France, Belgium and Holland eventually put London beyond the range of the V1 bombs. It was obvious to all by now that the war would soon be over. Yet Hitler was determined to carry on his revenge bombing of England. A team of German physicists under Werner von Braun had developed a missile bomb which they called the A4, and which would become known to England as the V2. The cost of each of these bombs was prohibitive: an estimated £1,200 as opposed to £125 for the V1s. And so, until the V1 was rendered powerless Hitler did not consider their use.

These rocket bombs reached speeds of 1,500 mph, weighed 4½ tons, ascended to a height of 120 miles and came down to explode unseen – the first that was known of them was as they hit. Tests on the bomb had shown that even without the explosive in the warhead the impact would cause a crater thirty to forty yards wide and ten to fifteen yards deep. Hitler ordered their mass production.

The first V2 was launched on 8 September 1944 and landed at Chiswick, West London. In all 1,403 would be launched with 1,054 falling on mainland Britain. Of these, 517 landed on London and 537 in eleven other counties. In terms of casualties the V2s were relatively ineffective, causing 2,514 deaths, but as a terror weapon they were unsurpassed. Explosions continued to lay low whole city blocks without warning right through until 27 March 1945 – eight days before the end of the war. At last the bombing was over.

The Blitz had a number of consequences, the most immediate and obvious being the British Strategic Bombing Offensive against Germany. Air Marshal Harris said of the Blitz, 'They have sown the wind, and they will reap the whirlwind.' By late 1941 Harris had organized the first 1,000 bomber raids over Germany. During the course of the war,

RAF Bomber Command in conjunction with the USAAF 8th Air Force would drop nineteen times the tonnage of explosive on Germany that the *Luftwaffe* had dropped on Britian. Whole cities would be laid waste, hundreds of thousands would die. In Hamburg alone 88,000 are estimated to have died in one raid. Comparing this to the total fatalities in Great Britain between 1939–1945 of 60,595 killed, it is easy to understand the sentiments of Divisional Officer Cyril Demarne when he heard of the destruction of Hamburg. Demarne says that he could not rejoice; he thought of the German firemen, of the women and children buried in their homes. Sub-Officer Wilmott was attached to the Allied occupation forces in Germany after the war and comments, 'We didn't know what bombing was.'

The bombing of the City of London gave an unequalled opportunity to City planners, such as had not been offered since the Great Fire of 1666. Whole areas lay flat and fallow, inviting creative reconstruction. As in 1666 so in 1945 – they blew it. St Paul's, before the war crowded in by office blocks allowing no good view, was to be treated with contempt. The modernist Juxon House on Ludgate Hill was allowed to block the view of the cathedral looking up the hill. At Paternoster Square a group of dedicated Portland cement *aficionados* constructed the revolting Paternoster Precinct – recently described by the Chief City Planning Officer as 'an urban desert'. Only now, some forty-five years later, have we become collectively aware of the horrors we have wrought – Paternoster Square is to be redeveloped in a style more befitting the neighbouring cathedral. Yet even now we are planning (as at the Mappin and Webb site in Poultry) the destruction of the few architectural gems left untouched by the *Luftwaffe*. All in all, it is an unedifying tale.

Little can be seen today in London to remind us of the Blitz. It can no longer be assumed, as it could until about ten years ago, that a new building occupies a bomb site. Now even the post-war buildings are coming down in the City's frenetic redevelopment. Yet there are reminders here and there to the observant visitor. Buildings throughout London still display chunks punched out of their stonework by the bombs. At St Clement Danes church on Fleet Street a fan of shrapnel holes from an HE bomb scar the wall of the church. Inside this church – the Central Church of the RAF – the floor is lined with the Squadron badges of more than 600 squadrons of the RAF and Polish, Indian, Pakistan, Canadian, New Zealand and Australian air forces, all of which fought the great battle in the skies over southern England.

Finally, a reminder that it had all happened before. The church of St Edmund the Martyr on Lombard Street has a display case with the remains of the Zeppelin bomb which came through the roof in 1917; and at Cleopatra's Needle on the Embankment, the bronze sphinxes are still perforated by shrapnel from a First World War bomb.

AFTERWORD
Richard T Jones
Director City Walks and Tours Ltd

London is one of the world's oldest and most fascinating cities. But, like many great cities, the real London can only be discovered by those adventurous enough to stroll away from the well-trodden tourist magnets.

At City Walks we have endeavoured over the years to provide a relaxed, informative way for people to explore London. Most of those who take our tours comment on how much they have learned. Credit for this must go to our guides, particularly those who contributed to this book. It is their enthusiasm and extensive knowledge on all aspects of London's history that make our walks so popular. Our guides are not given a script to recite: they are people who have studied their subjects for years and, more importantly, who can put over their knowledge in a way that is entertaining to hear.

I hope we will have the opportunity of sharing London with you in the future, and hope that this book will inspire you to discover more of our great city.

Richard T Jones
London, 1990